James Warner
(1817-1869)

WARNER
CIVIL WAR
CAVALRY CARBINES

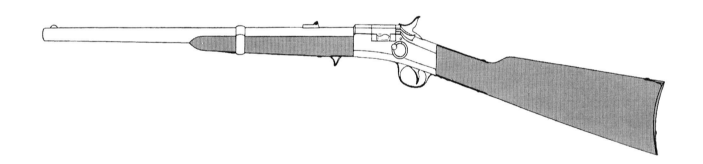

Col. J. Alan Hassell USAF (Ret)

Edited by Roy M. Marcot and Edward A. Hull

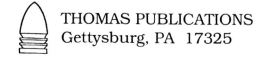

THOMAS PUBLICATIONS
Gettysburg, PA 17325

Copyright © 2000 J. Alan Hassell

Printed and bound in the United States of America

Published by THOMAS PUBLICATIONS
        P.O. Box 3031
        Gettysburg, Pa. 17325

ISBN-1-57747-063-X

Cover design by Ryan C. Stouch

To
Carole, Kristen & Colin

TABLE OF CONTENTS

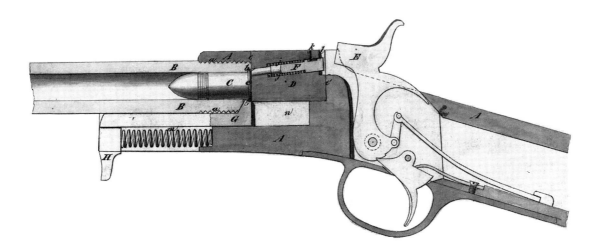

IN APPRECIATION

To my wife Carole. Twenty years ago she suggested I limit my gun collecting to Civil War carbines. Little could she have known that it would lead to my writing a book about James Warner's breech loaders.

To my long time friend John Newstead of Norwich, England. His talent in locating Warner carbines was instrumental in generating my interest about their history and that of their inventor.

To Margret "Maggie" Humberston of the Connecticut Valley Historical Museum. Her superb ability to uncover new information on the life of James Warner formed the foundation for the writing of the prologue.

To Michael Musick of the National Archives. His instruction on how to properly research material and assistance in locating important information within that facility was of immense help.

To Stu Vogt, former curator of firearms at the Springfield Armory Museum, and Melodie Kosmacki of the Smithsonian Museum. Their assistance in permitting close examinations of Warner carbines in their museum collections is greatly appreciated.

To Warner pistol collectors — Lee Arbuckle and Henry Truslow. Their assistance in providing photographs of Warner pistols from their collections was an immense help in completing the book.

To Marian (Warner) Bates and Joe Warner, great grandchildren of James Warner. Their kindness in providing family photographs and detailed information on James Warner and his family was invaluable.

To Roy Marcot and Edward Hull. Their detailed edit of the manuscript, thoughtful comments and recommendations did much to improve the overall quality of this work.

To Patrick White for his drawing of James Warner's Longmeadow Road factory circa 1865.

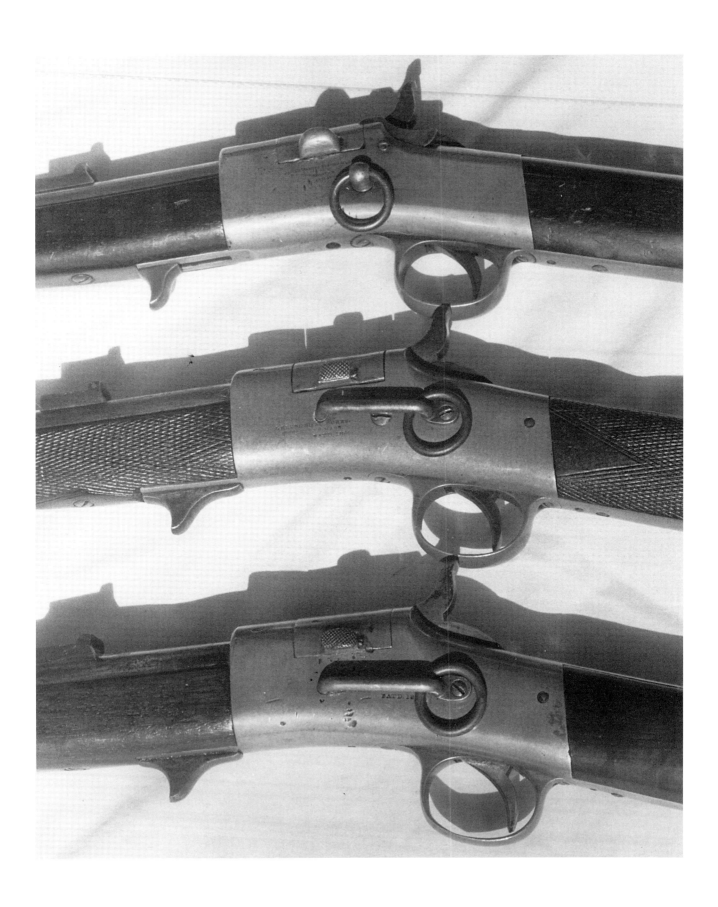

PREFACE

As a boy I received my first American Civil War carbine, a Smith, from my father. Ever since, I have had a keen interest in learning more about these short-barreled breechloaders used by Union cavalry units during the Civil War. Over the years my collection has grown and with it the number of Warner carbines has also increased.

A three-year assignment with the United States Air Force in Washington, D.C., provided the opportunity to visit the National Archives to find out more about James Warner and his contracts with the United States government. Naively, I thought a visit or two to the Archives would be sufficient time to complete the needed research. This idea was quickly dispelled when I realized that a substantial amount of information existed. The only trouble was locating it. Soon I found myself spending evenings, weekends and vacations sitting in the central research room poring over literally thousands of original documents attempting to find those pertaining to Warner's carbine. As each piece of the puzzle was set in place and a picture began to emerge, my desire to understand the complete story of James Warner also increased. Soon I was dragging my wife on research trips to Massachusetts, Pennsylvania, and Florida to photograph old warehouse buildings, examine carbines and conduct interviews.

As my research expanded it became clear that much of the limited amount of information previously written about Warner and his carbines was incorrect. Faulty assumptions and unsubstantiated conclusions by early authors had been perpetuated in later works as fact. In a concerted effort to avoid making a similar mistake, I decided to write this book using original first source documentation whenever possible. Generalizations were entirely avoided, and logical conclusions supported by hard documentation were clearly identified as such. My goal, therefore, became to write a book based entirely on thorough research and exhaustive documentation, and create a solid reference work for future generations. I hope I have been successful in achieving that objective.

Alan Hassell

PROLOGUE

James Warner: The Early Years

In the mid 1800s, the area between Springfield, Massachusetts, and New Haven, Connecticut, was the hub of the arms-making industry in the United States. Concentrated in close proximity to the National Armory at Springfield and along the Connecticut River Valley were the major arms companies of Samuel Colt, Christian Sharps and Eli Whitney. Other smaller companies competing for a part of the growing market in small arms were the Massachusetts Arms Company and Smith and Wesson, to mention a few. One less heralded concern was the Springfield Arms Company.

James Warner was born just north of Springfield in South Hadley, Massachusetts, on May 16, 1817.[1] The son of Daniel and Azubah Collins Warner, he had two brothers, Daniel and Charles, and one sister, Clarissa. His family name, familiar in the Connecticut River Valley, could be traced as far back as 1637 to William Warner of Ipswich, Massachusetts.[2]

James was a cousin to Thomas Warner,[3] an experienced gunmaker who worked at the National Armory from 1810-1843, eventually attaining the position of chief armorer. Thomas left the National Armory in 1843 to work for Samuel Colt and by 1847 was the superintendent of the Colt "Walker" project in Eli Whitney's armory at Whitneyville, Connecticut. In 1849, hired by the Massachusetts Arms Company of Chicopee Falls, he set up a plant to produce arms covered by the Wesson and Leavitt patents.[4]

During the period of Thomas' employment at Whitneyville, twenty nine year old James Warner is first found listed as a Colt company workman at the forging works of Slate & Brown in Windsor-Locks, Connecticut. His job was rough turning and boring "Walker" pistol cylinders and barrels for the wage of $1.50 a day.[5]

While employed at Windsor-Locks, James married Eleanor Scrugham, a student at Mount Holyoke College just outside of South Hadley.[6] Born in New York City on February 15, 1824, Eleanor was the daughter of William Warburton and Elizabeth Burnett Scrugham.[7] Her father had immigrated from Dublin, Ireland, in 1810 and opened a dry goods store in the lower part of New York City. She and her older brother William Warburton Scrugham (1820-1867) lost both of their parents at an early age, thereby making William the sole means of Eleanor's support. Despite this hardship, William eventually graduated from Columbia College in 1843, moved to Yonkers, New York and established his credentials as a lawyer and junior member of a law practice in White Plains, New York. In 1849, William was appointed a lieutenant colonel in the 7th Regiment of State Militia and eventually rose to the rank of brigadier general. Ten years later, in 1859, he was elected a Justice of the New York State Supreme Court. Later that year he married Miss Mary Killinger, also of Yonkers, New York.[8]

Family legend has it that Eleanor and James Warner eloped. Whatever the circumstances, they were married in Lebanon Springs, New York on May 22, 1843.[9] The 1850 Springfield City Directory mentions that he resided on Gardner Street in Springfield with his wife, four year old daughter Eleanor and newborn son Warburton. That year their three year old son James died.[10] Also in 1850, Warner purchased a house for $1,000 on Blake's Hill (now Woodside Terrace). In a possible effort to assist with finances and provide Warner more capital for his growing business, William Warburton Scrugham purchased the property in March 1851 for $1,000 and quickly deeded it back to Eleanor "in consideration of love and affection and one dollar...."[11] The bond between William and Eleanor must have been strong, for this would not be the last time William rendered financial assistance to James Warner and his family.

Judge William W. Scrugham.
(Connecticut Valley Historical Museum)

Warner family c. 1867. Left to right: Robert, Eleanor Virginia (standing), George, James Jr., James, Kate, Warburton (standing), Eleanor, Harry.   (Bates family collection)

The Warner household continued to grow with another son, Robert, being born in 1854, a third son, James, three years later and in 1858, a second daughter, Catherine. By 1860, it is obvious that James Warner had achieved a substantial degree of success and had become firmly established in the Springfield community. A copy of his U.S. Federal Census Return for that year indicated that the forty-two year old pistol manufacturer had a family of seven, plus a laborer, servant and bookkeeper, all residing at his residence at Blake's Hill. Additionally, his personal worth was listed as the quite respectable amount (for the time) of $10,000.[12] By 1864, his family had grown to nine, with a son, George, being born in 1862, and another son, Harry, born two years later.

Springfield Arms Company

The first mention of James Warner's arms production ability was a listing in the 1850 Springfield City Directory for "Warner, James (& Co.), Pistol Factory, Lyman Street". It is from this facility that he probably manufactured revolvers of the Elijah Jaquith patent.[13] Sometime between 1851-1852 he relocated his factory to South Main Street. By 1852, James Warner was

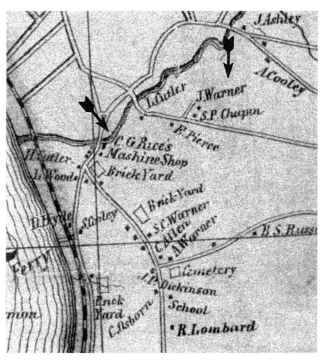

City map of Springfield, Mass. c. 1855. Note James Warner's residence (arrow) and C.G. Rice's building. The "machine shop" next to Rice's place could be the location of the Springfield Arms Company as mentioned in the 1851-1852 Springfield City Directory.

(Connecticut Valley Historical Museum)

UNITED STATES PATENT OFFICE.

JAMES WARNER, OF SPRINGFIELD, MASSACHUSETTS.

IMPROVEMENT IN REVOLVING-BREECH FIRE-ARMS.

Specification forming part of Letters Patent No. 8,229, dated July 15, 1851.

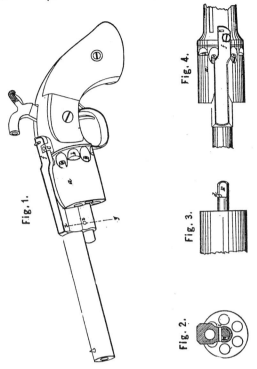

To all whom it may concern:

Be it known that I, JAMES WARNER, of Springfield, county of Hampden, State of Massachusetts, have invented certain Improvements in the Construction of Repeating Fire-Arms; and I do declare the following to be a full, clear, and exact description of the same, reference being made to the annexed drawings, forming part of the same, in which—

Figure I is a view in perspective of my improvements. Figs. II, III, and IV are parts in detail; and similar letters refer to similar parts throughout the figures.

My invention relates to certain improvements in revolving arms, whereby a superior method is attained of effecting the attaching and detaching of the barrels from their stocks.

My invention consists in the engagement and disengagement of the barrel from the stock. This is effected with great facility in my improvements by merely slackening up a screw in the stock, attached near the end of the back strap of the barrel, when a quarter-revolution of the barrel will immediately release it from the stock. To accomplish this I affix a stud, c, having a square head, upon the stock. This stud is placed a little to one side of the central line or sight of the piece. In the side of the back brace-piece or strap, f, there is a notch cut to fit around the pin c, as clearly shown in Figs. I and IV. The top of the pin is flush with the surface of the brace, and has besides a hole drilled and tapped to receive a screw. This screw is seen in Fig. IV, and when screwed down its head, being larger than the top of the stud, presses upon the strap and prevents any movement of the barrel. The barrel outside of the revolving chamber is supported upon the end of the pin upon which they revolve by means of the hole drilled in

the lower end of the brace. In the old mode, to keep this part steady a hole is drilled through both the brace and pin and a key or screw inserted. My fastening differs from this. The end of the shaft is cut with a notch, as seen in Fig. III at letter D. One side of the pin is then cut to form a flat surface extending from the notch out to the end, as seen at e, Figs. II and III. A small pin is driven through the brace at i, Figs. I and II, and firmly riveted in it, so that it cannot be moved. When the barrel is set in place this pin i fills the notch d, and consequently, together with the stud c, holds the barrel in place.

To remove the barrel the screw on c must be slightly slackened, as it is not necessary to take it out, and the barrel being turned round until the little pin i comes opposite to the place where the notch is cut away at e, it can then be pulled off. The stud c being a little to one side of the sight, the side of the strap f, in being turned slightly, rises up. The head of the screw therefore must be raised sufficiently to allow the strap to pass from under. Therefore, when screwed hard down, it prevents the barrel from turning or being misplaced.

What I claim as of my own invention, and desire to secure by Letters Patent of the United States, is—

The arrangement for securing the barrel to the stock—viz., the combination of the stud c with the notch in the back strap, f, and with the notch d and pin i, as described, the whole being constructed and operating substantially as set forth herein.

JAMES WARNER.

Witnesses:
LEWIS FOSTER,
C. A. FISK.

Warner's 1851 revolver patent, number 8229.   (National Archives)

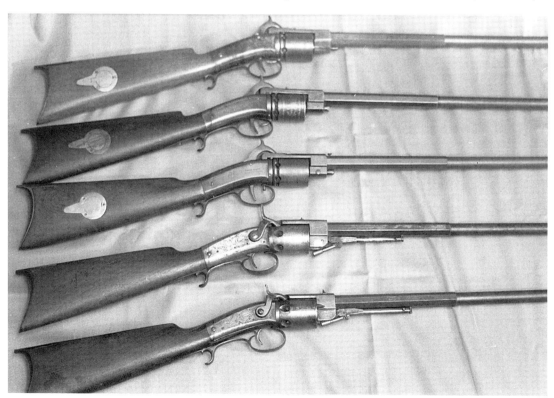

Warner Open Frame Revolving Carbines based on Patent No. 8229. Top three are similar to first model pistols while bottom two are similar to second model Dragoon pistols. Circa early 1850s.

(Henry Stewart Collection)

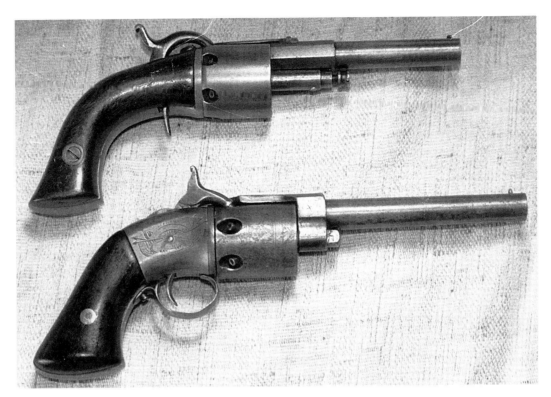

Top: Springfield Arms Co. Prototype First Model Open Frame Pistol.
Bottom: Springfield Arms Co., Warner Patent Belt Model, Serial No. 52. Marked "Warner's Patent/Jan 1851" on right side of frame and "Springfield Arms Co." on top strap. (Henry Truslow collection)

Very scarce James Warner Pocket Pistol No. 526 boxed with all accessories. Dealer label reads, "A. McComas, Maker and Importer of Guns, Rifles and Pistols; 31 Calvert St., Baltimore." Cylinder is marked twice "James Warner — Springfield, Mass." This is a transitional model being one of the earliest made under Warner's name and has characteristics of the Springfield Arms Co. Fourth model pocket pistols. (Henry Truslow Collection)

JAMES WARNER,
MANUFACTURER OF
PATENT REVOLVING
BREECH RIFLES AND PISTOLS,
SPRINGFIELD, MASS.
☞ Orders respectfully solicted.

Springfield Arms Co. advertising in Bessey's Springfield Directory 1856-1857.   (Connecticut Valley Historical Museum)

listed as Agent and Superintendent for the newly formed Springfield Arms Company located next to the concern of Charles G. Rice, an established lead pipe and pump manufacturer.[14]

The South Main Street factory probably was the location where the Springfield Arms Company pistol manufacturing occurred. The Trade and Industry section of the 1851-52 Springfield City Directory gives some insight into the size and capability of the pistol works.

---

140   SPRINGFIELD TRADE

We are not aware of the annual amount of production.

D. PERKINS'S, MACHINE SHOP.
Situated on Mill river, opposite C. G. Rice's Lead Pipe and Pump Shop, where he carries on all kinds of making and repairing machinery. He has got a good set of new tools such as screw cutting and turning engines, hand lathes, a power planeing machine and other tools usually kept for the business. He also makes and repairs whips and other braiding machines.

SPRINGFIELD ARMS COMPANY.
This is a new establishment, and one of much interest and importance. The building is situated a few rods above Rice's building. The articles manufactured are Warner's Patent Revolver pistols and carbines. They are the invention of James Warner, formerly of South Hadley, who is the agent of the company, and the arms are certainly among the simplest and most efficient of all revolvers yet invented. The first facts apparent in their construction are that they can be discharged with the same rapidity as Colt's, and with the same efficiency. They are also no less light and beautiful in construction, and Mr. Warner claims that they are more simple and of course less liable to get out of repair. Six discharges can be made in from 8 to 10 seconds. The building is furnished with $20,000 worth of new machinery, consisting of 15 engine lathes, planing machines, upright lathes, and all the appurtenances of a pistol factory. The number of hands employed is 60. The carbines are capital arms for deer and bear hunting at the West and South. The number of pistols turned out daily, some of which are finished in the highest style, is 26. We are glad to learn that the sale is so rapid that hardly a specimen ean be kept for exhibition.

Springfield City Directory 1851-1852, Trade & Industry, Section D, Page 140. (Connecticut Valley Historical Museum)

SPRINGFIELD ARMS COMPANY.

This is a new establishment, and one of much interest and importance. The building is situated a few rods above Rice's building. The articles manufactured are Warner's Patent Revolver pistols and carbines. They are the invention of James Warner, formerly of South Hadley, who is the agent of the company, and the arms are certainly among the simplest and most efficient of all revolvers yet invented. The first facts apparent in their construction are that they can be discharged with the same rapidity as Colt's, and with the same efficiency. They are also no less light and beautiful in construction, and Mr. Warner claims that they are more simple and of course less liable to get out of repair. Six discharges can be made in from 8 to 10 seconds. The building is furnished with $20,000 worth of new machinery, consisting of 15 engine lathes, planing machines, upright lathes, and all the appurtenances of a pistol factory. The number of hands employed is 60. The carbines are capital arms for deer and bear hunting at the West and South. The number of pistols turned out daily, some of which are finished in the highest style, is 26. We are glad to learn that the sale is so rapid that hardly a specimen can be kept for exhibition.

WARNER'S
NEW MODEL POCKET REVOLVER.

(THIS ENGRAVING IS THE EXACT SIZE OF THE REVOLVER.)

REVOLVES BY COCKING.

THIS Pistol, for durability and simplicity of construction, stands unrivaled in the world. It has always been a serious objection to rotating breech fire-arms, that the great number of parts used in their construction, and many of them being frail, made them extremely liable to fail at a time when they should be most depended upon. In this Pistol, this defect is almost entirely overcome, there being less pieces used in its construction than there are even in an ordinary single barrel pistol, and they being of the most durable kind.

DIRECTIONS FOR LOADING AND CLEANING.

IN loading it is not necessary to use either patch or wad, the ball being driven down perfectly tight upon the powder. To detach the cylinder (A) from the pistol, draw the hammer (B) to half-cock, screw out the pin (C), draw the lever (D), to which is attached the base pin upon which the cylinder rotates, and then press the cylinder to the right, turning it at the same time.

To replace the cylinder, put it in the frame from the right, pressing back the lever which rotates it.

Clean well the cylinder and base-pin after use, care being taken to have both thoroughly dried and oiled after cleaning.

JAMES WARNER,
SPRINGFIELD,
MASS.

James Warner, Springfield, Mass. Advertising Broadside c. 1850s. Original is with black lettering on light blue paper.   (Henry Truslow Collection)

UNITED STATES PATENT OFFICE.

JAMES WARNER, OF SPRINGFIELD, MASSACHUSETTS.

IMPROVEMENT IN REVOLVING FIRE-ARMS.

Specification forming part of Letters Patent No. **17,904**, dated July 28, 1857.

J. WARNER.

Revolver.

No. 17,904.

Patented July 28, 1857.

To all whom it may concern:

Be it known that I, JAMES WARNER, of Springfield, county of Hampden, and State of Massachusetts, have invented a certain new and useful Improvement in Revolving Fire-Arms; and I do hereby declare that the following is a full, clear, and exact description of the same, reference being made to the annexed drawings, making a part of this specification, in which—

Figure I is a side elevation, partly in section. Fig. II is of a part in detail.

Similar letters indicate similar parts in both the figures.

My improvement is applicable only to those repeating fire-arms wherein the revolution of the charge-cylinder is effected by the point of a lever which projects through the shield-plate, taking into a series of ratchet-grooves on the rear end of the cylinder, and which lever is required to retreat, as a latch, in a somewhat horizontal direction in order to take a new hold for the next rotative movement. As usually constructed this act of retreating is permitted by having a slot instead of a circular hole for that pin to act in which confines the reverse end of the lever, and thus the lever may have the necessary longitudinal movement. A coiled spring is so affixed that it will draw the point of the lever toward the cylinder, and this arrangement effects the purpose very well when the parts are new and clean; but when from the piece being fouled after repeated firing the rotation is rendered more difficult the point of the lever is apt, particularly when it has become slightly worn, to slip out or be unlatched in the act of cocking, and since the rotation is effected by the cocking the piece will not then be discharged for the reason that the rotation will have been but a partial one. To keep the lever forward under these circumstances some device is required which shall be more positive in its action than the spring alone. For the purpose merely of giving a rotation with certainty all that is necessary would be that the lever should have freedom simply to turn upon the pin at the back end, the slid-

ing motion along it being essential only when the lever is returned in the act of firing, in order that it may ride over the edge of the next groove below to take a new hold. My construction is such that the lever will be held firmly in the advanced position—that is, the centering-pin being then in the back end of the slot—during all the time that a rotation is being effected by the said lever, and will be free to slide along the pin when in the act of passing to the next groove. I effect this by cutting away the back end of the slot *a* in the lever *b*, so as to form a depression which will receive into it about one-half of the pin *c*, confining that end, and, as shown clearly in the enlarged view, Fig. II.

The operation will be that as the piece is being fired the pin *i*, which extends, as seen in Fig. I, from the hammer into a slot in the lever *b*, carries that point of the lever downward which is in contact with the cylinder, and in so doing will also have a tendency to depress the reverse end, and therefore the pin will then have a bearing against the upper side of the curved slot, and the lever can readily take the backward movement necessary to allow it to pass into the next catch in the cylinder, as in Fig. I it is represented as about to. On cocking again the pin *i* acts to lift both ends of the lever *b*, and the coiled spring having again drawn the lever forward the pin *c* will now rest in the depression. The bearing of the lever up against it is sufficient to keep the lever from slipping off, and hence the point cannot retreat to escape from the catch in which it is engaged, thus insuring the accurate revolving of the cylinder to the full extent required.

I claim—

The specific device in the end of the slot for preventing the retreat of the lever *b* in the act of cocking, substantially as set forth herein.

JAMES WARNER.

Witnesses:
S. H. MAYNARD,
THOMAS DUCEY.

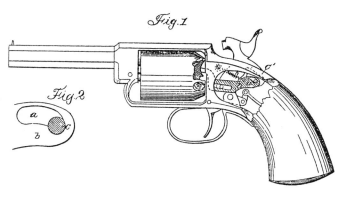

Warner's 1857 revolver patent, number 17904.   (National Archives)

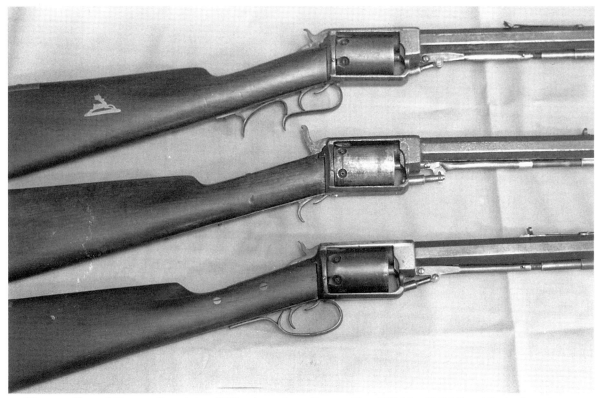

Warner Closed Frame Revolving Rifles based on Patent No. 17904. (Middle rifle lacks trigger guard.) Circa mid to late 1850s.

(Henry Stewart Collection)

James Warner, Springfield, Mass. Second Model Solid Frame Pocket Revolvers showing different engraving patterns on frame and ivory grips.

(Henry Truslow Collection)

Cased James Warner Pocket Cartridge Pistol. Gutta Percha case lined with red velvet. Revolver is 5 shot, .30 caliber fitted with a 3-inch barrel and a frame with a loading gate on the right side.   (Lee Arbuckle Collection; George Martin photo)

Longmeadow Road Operations

By 1857, Warner had established a partnership with Albert Morgan and had acquired a parcel of land just south of the Springfield-Longmeadow town line where the Longmeadow Road crosses Pecousic Brook.[15] This location must have had good potential for a factory site, for in February 1859, they took over a mortgage for a second adjoining property.[16]

Warner's problems began to come to a head in 1862. He no more than introduced his new model solid frame cartridge revolver when Smith and Wesson took him to court with a patent infringement suit.[17] Things got progressively worse in 1863 with the death of Albert Morgan[18] and a judgment against him in the patent suit. As a result of the court decision, Warner was required

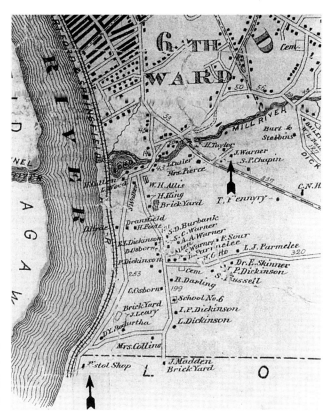

(Right) City map of Springfield, Mass. c. 1864. Note James Warner's residence just south of Mill River (arrow) and his pistol shop (Longmeadow Road Factory) at bottom of map. (Connecticut Valley Historical Museum)

James Warner's Longmeadow Road Factory c. 1880's. (Connecticut Valley Historical Museum)

to return to Smith and Wesson the 1,513 revolvers that had not yet been sold. This marked the end of the Springfield Arms Company.[19]

Following the demise of the Springfield Arms Company, Warner once again sought the aid of his brother-in-law in order to obtain enough capital to renew his arms making business. The now Judge William W. Scrugham agreed to his proposal and lent Warner $10,500[20] to facilitate a move to a new factory on the Longmeadow Road. This relocation is confirmed by a Springfield City Directory entry in 1864 and again in 1865 listing "James Warner, Pistol Manufacturer, Longmeadow Road,(home) Blake Hill." It is from this factory that his brass frame breechloading carbines marked "James Warner, Springfield Mass" were manufactured and supplied to the federal government.

Warner must have found that the workload of setting up his new Longmeadow Road factory and manufacturing carbines in the quantity the government desired exceeded both his personal ability and that of his factory. To assist him, Warner enlisted Everett Hosmer Barney of Boston. Barney was an inventor in his own right and had in 1864 Patented the idea of fastening ice skates to a shoe by a metal clamp, thus dispensing with the old method of leather straps and buckles.[21]

The Greene Rifle Works

To assist in meeting production deadlines, Warner also obtained the assistance of the Greene Rifle Works of Worcester, Massachusetts. They were located in the Junction Shop, a three-story, 450 foot long stone building located just north of the Junction Station on the Norwich and Worcester and Western Railroads[22] and only one block from both the Ballard and Allen and Wheelock arms factories.

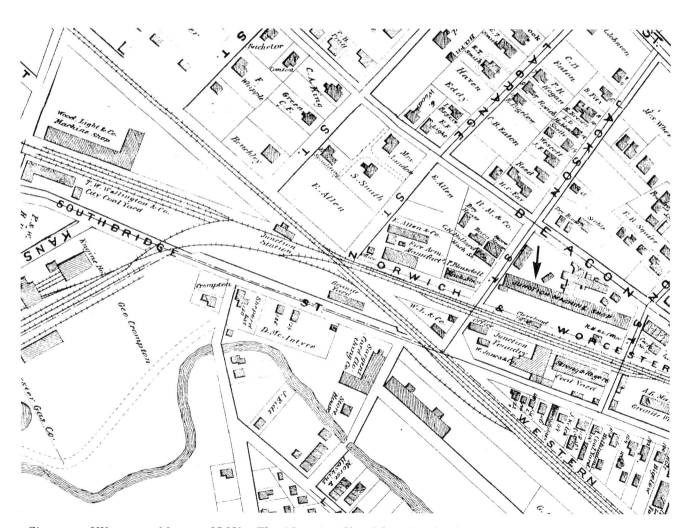

City map of Worcester, Mass. c. 1860's. The "Junction Shop" housing the Greene Rifle Works is between Herman and Jackson Streets (arrow). The firms of C.H. Ballard and Ethan Allen are between Jackson and LaGrange Streets.

This facility had been erected in 1853 by James Estabrook with the financial backing of Eli Thayer. In 1859, B.F. Joslyn and his agent William C. Freeman purchased the structure from Thayer and subsequently began production of Joslyn's patented pistols, as well as parts for his percussion breechloading carbines.[23]

Joslyn relocated his factory operations to Stonington, Connecticut, in 1861 and the Junction Shop was, it is believed, taken over by James W. Emery following his purchase of the patent and manufacturing interests of Lieutenant Colonel J. Durrell Greene for an oval bore, underhammer, percussion breechloading rifle.[24] By 1863, it must have become readily apparent to Emery that further government contracts for the Greene percussion rifle would not be forthcoming. This made him both available and eager to produce other model arms.

Warner, on the other hand, needed help. His Longmeadow Road Factory was either not yet completed or unable to produce carbines fast enough to meet the delivery requirements of his government contract. Accordingly, on October 1, 1863 Warner subcontracted with the Greene Rifle Works to assist in the manufacture of his carbine.[25] It is from this facility that Warner's "improved model" breechloading carbines, marked "Greene Rifle Works, Worcester Mass, 1864," originated.

CHAPTER 1

PATENTS

A New Start

Following the loss of the patent infringement suit with Smith & Wesson, James Warner began active design of his breechloading carbine. By the spring of 1863, he had perfected his design and submitted his patent to Munn and Company in New York City, who would act as his attorneys in presenting his application to the U.S. Patent Office. The patent office received his application on March 2, 1863. This consisted of a petition, affidavit, specification, 2 drawings (actual size) and a model.[1]

Breech loading Carbine Patent

To all whom it may concern:
Be it known that I, James Warner of Springfield in the County of Hamden, and State of Massachusetts, have invented a new and useful improvement in Breech loading firearms.

The invention relates to that construction of breech loading firearms in which the breech opens with a swinging movement about an axis situated at one side of the frame and parallel with the bore of the barrel. It consists firstly in a novel construction of such breech and of that part of the frame of the arm which receives it whereby while the strength of the frame is retained in the greatest possible degree, great convenience is afforded for loading with fixed ammunition. In order to provide for the firing, the breech is fitted like the breeches of some other breech loading firearms with a sliding firing pin on which the hammer strikes to drive it against the portion of the shell of the ammunition which contains the priming. The pin has applied to it a spiral spring to draw it back within the breech and a stop screw to prevent it from being withdrawn back by the spring further than necessary. A second feature of the invention consists in a certain arrangement and combination of

the said sliding pin, the hammer and a recess in the back of the breech, whereby when the breech is closed and the hammer down, the hammer is made to lock the breech securely.

James Warner

Problems with Washington

By the end of March, Munn & Company received word from the U.S. Patent Office that Warner's application had been disapproved.[2]

James Warner
Care of Munn & Company
New York   March 30, 1863

Sir
Your application for patent—Breech loading firearm has been examined and not found to present any patentable novelty. For the subject of your first claim see the patent of D. Minesinger February 27, 1849 and the rejected applications of Moore and Hall rejected September 8, 1854 and of J.W. Wilkinson filed December 17, 1861. For the subject of your second claim, see the patents of Ethan Allen September 18, 1860 and of S.W. Wood April 1, 1862 Figure 14. Your application must therefore be refused. Your specifications and drawing are herewith returned.
Respectfully
William B. T.

During April, Warner and the Munn Company attorneys worked to amend his patent specification by removing all reference to the breechblock "spring bolt" mechanism which held the breechblock closed against accidental opening. Additionally, his original two-part claim was replaced with the following single claim:[3]

The construction of the semicylindrical recess of a diameter corresponding to that of the flange of the metallic cartridge, in combination with the semicylindrical breech piece projection, the recess and the hammer as herein shown and described; so that when the breech piece is open the cartridge case will be guided in an exact line with the barrel both in loading and withdrawing the case; and when the breech piece is closed the solid portion thereof, or semicylindrical projection will press against the rear of the cartridge shell, while the fall of the hammer will lock the breech piece and prevent it from being blown open by the accidental rearward bursting of the shell; the premature discharge or striking of the hammer upon the cartridge pin being also avoided, all as set forth.

By the following month he was ready to resubmit his application:[4]

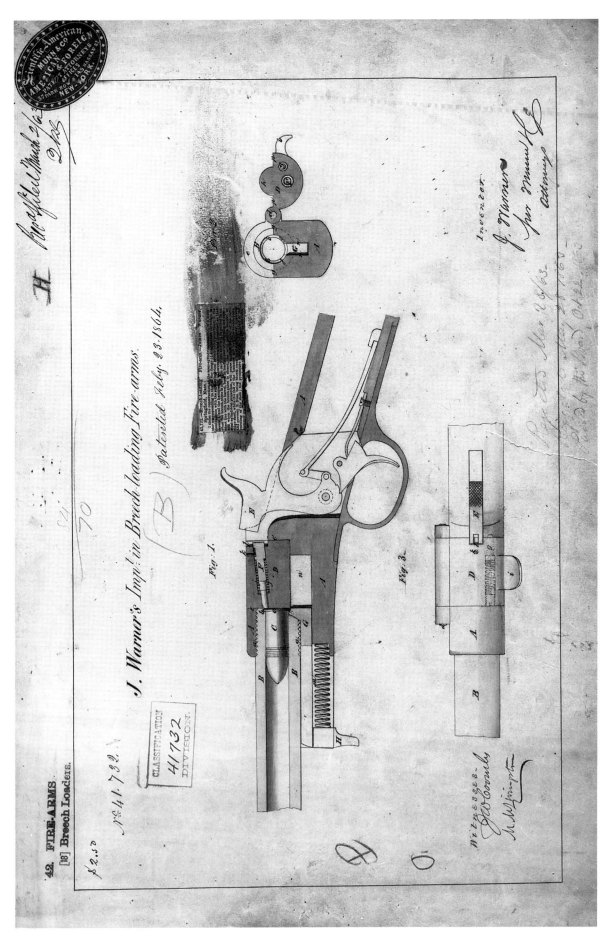

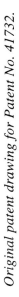

Original patent drawing for Patent No. 41732.

Patent model for Patent No. 41732, Serial No. 3.   (Springfield Armory Museum Collection)

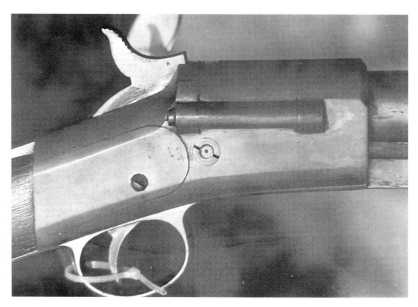

Right side of Warner model carbine receiver Serial No. 3. Note cover plate lacks slot to insert screwdriver blade to facilitate removal and crude style saddle ring bolt nut.   (Springfield Armory Museum Collection)

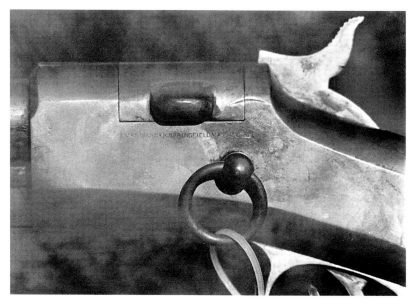

Serial No. 3: Receiver marking "James Warner, Springfield, Mass., USA." Note normal contour of Warner model arms receiver and presence of the normal sling ring and bolt. Note lack of a breech block catsh mechanism found on standard Warner model carbines. Breech block locking mechanism is contained within the breech block itself.

(Springfield Armory Museum Collection)

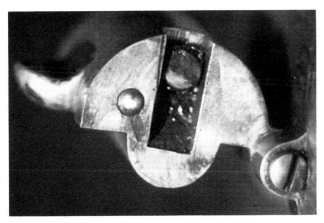

Rear face of breech block clearly shows rounded head of spring-loaded plunger which fits into a recess in the receiver and thereby holds breech block closed when hammer is not fully forward. (Springfield Armory Museum Collection)

Front face of breech block marked "Warner's Patent." Screw permits access to coil spring and plunger mechanism. It should be noted that the breech block mechanism of this patent is similar to but not identical with that used in Greene model arms.

(Springfield Armory Museum Collection)

Warner "Patent Model" carbine, Serial No. 3, using Springfield model 1861 rifle, type 2 leaf rear sight.

(Springfield Armory Museum Collection)

Office of the Scientific American
37 Park Row
New York   May 8, 1863
Hon. Commissioner of Patents

Sir:

Herewith we return the specification drawing of J. Warners firearm with amendment. A reconsideration is respectfully asked.

If the claim or any part of the specification is inadmissible we shall feel obliged by the suggestion of such a change as will probably meet the views of the office.

Munn & Company

However, Warner's luck was not to change. By the end of May the Patent Office disapproved his second application:[5]

James Warner
c/o Munn & Co.
New York   May 28, 1863

Sir;

On a reexamination of your application for patent Breech loading firearm, the Office perceives nothing in your amended claim filed the 13th inst presenting any essential novelty. Wilkinson hammer locks the hinged breech block by means of the nipple, as effectively as yours does by its recess in the breech block. The rejected application of W.O. Hickok filed January 17, 1862 also locks the swinging breech by the nose of the hammer. Your application is therefore a second time rejected.

Respectfully,
William B. T.

This second rejection still did not discourage Warner. Within two weeks he had amended his specification a second time. Upon refiling Munn & Company Attorneys enclosed a detailed appeal that supported the basis of Warners claim:[6]

Office of Munn & Co.
Scientific American Patent Agency
New York   June 16, 1863
To the Commissioner of Patents

Sir:

We return to the files the Specification Amendment and one drawing of J. Warner Improvement in Fire Arms.

Respectfully,
Munn & Co.
Attorneys

Success at Last

Apparently, the attorneys at Munn & Company had done their research well and presented their case effectively. This was evidenced by the findings of the Patent Office Examiner-in-Chief dated September 28, 1863:[7]

> The alleged invention relates to that class of breech loading arm in which metallic flanged cartridge cases are used. In the rear of the barrel there is a hinged breech piece swinging laterally, which fits into a recess in the frame, long enough to admit the cartridge when said breech piece is swung open. In the lower part of said recess in the frame, there is a semicylindrical groove, concentric with the barrel, but of a diameter corresponding to that of the flange of the cartridge case, so that when the cartridge case is laid in said groove with it forward and inserted in the barrel it will be guided in an exact line with the barrel. On the lower side of said swinging breech block there is a semicylindrical projection, which, when the breech block is closed down exactly fits in said groove. The fulminate in the flange of the cartridge is ignited by means of a pin carried loosely in the breech block, the rear end of which receives the blow of the hammer, which drives it forward so that the front end will strike the flange of the cartridge case. In the rear end of such breech block, at the point where the hammer strikes there is a recess or notch which the face of the hammer enters, locking said breech piece so that it cannot be opened until the hammer is raised. The claim, as amended since first rejection, is to the combination of the semicylindrical groove, "of a diameter corresponding to that of the flange of the metallic cartridge", the semicylindrical projection on the breech piece, the recess in the breech piece into which the face of the hammer fits, to lock the breech piece, and the hammer. A number of references are given by the examiner, in none of which do we find the precise combination claimed. In one only (the patent of S.W. Wood) do we find a similar device to that of the applicant, for locking the breech piece by means of the hammer; and we do not find it here in connection with a groove like that of the applicant, for guiding the cartridge. In fact there is nothing in any of the references which fully answers to the said groove and the projection on the breech block which fits into it, as shown in the case of the applicant. It is observed that the references cited by the Examiner do not answer the claim of the applicant, and his decision is reversed.
>
> J.J. Coombs
> T.C. Theaker
> Examiner-in-Chief

James Warner's persistence had finally paid off, and his patent application had been approved. But his problems were still not over. On January 9, 1864 Munn & Co. received a letter from the Patent Office stating that they would be unable to process Warners application due to the fact that it had been mislaid, and that Munn & Co. would need to resubmit the specifications and amendments before a patent could be issued.[8] This was promptly accomplished on January 18, 1864. Finally, on February 23, 1864, one year after his original patent application was filed, James Warner was issued Patent No. 41,732.[9]

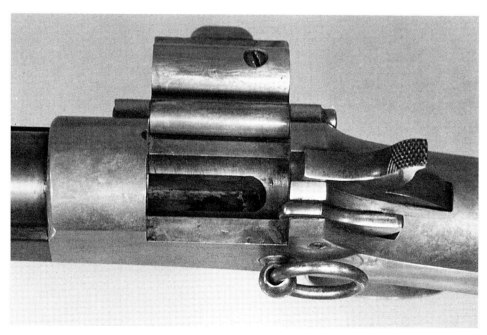

Illustration of Warner's claim in Patent No. 41732. Receiver with breech block opened clearly shows area milled to cradle cartridge. Note breech block "flipper" mechanism to left of hammer. (Smithsonian Collection)

Another Patent

One day prior to his first patent being issued, Warners application for what would eventually be his second patent for breechloading firearms, was received by the U.S. Patent Office:[10]

> To all whom it may concern -
> Be it known that I, James Warner of Springfield, in the county of Hamden and State of Massachusetts have invented certain new and useful improvements in Breechloading firearms.
> This invention consists firstly in a novel arrangement of a locking device in a closed condition, a breech block which opens and closes by a movement about an axis parallel with and on one side of the line of the bore of the barrel, whereby great facility is afforded for rapidly reloading. It consists secondly in certain novel means of producing the extraction of a pin which works through such a breech block as is above mentioned for the purpose of being struck by

the hammer to fire the charge, whereby the necessity for a spring in combination with said pin is obviated. It consists thirdly in a mode of supporting the extractor which is employed to withdraw the discharged metallic cartridge shells from the barrel, whereby that part of the flange of the shell which is received in the extractor is prevented from being burst in the firing and the extractor is prevented from slipping past the said flange in the withdrawal of the shell. The rear end of the locking lever projects upward in such a manner that after firing the operator may without relinquishing the grasp of his right hand, first half cock the hammer and then apply his thumb to press down the end of the lever by which means the front end of the lever is drawn out of the notch and the breech block unlocked. By swinging the arm over quickly on its right side the breech block will usually fall open, to permit the loading, the pressure of the left thumb against the thumb piece being only necessary in case of the breech block sticking. When the breech block is swung back into the cavity to close the chamber after loading, it presses against the rounded

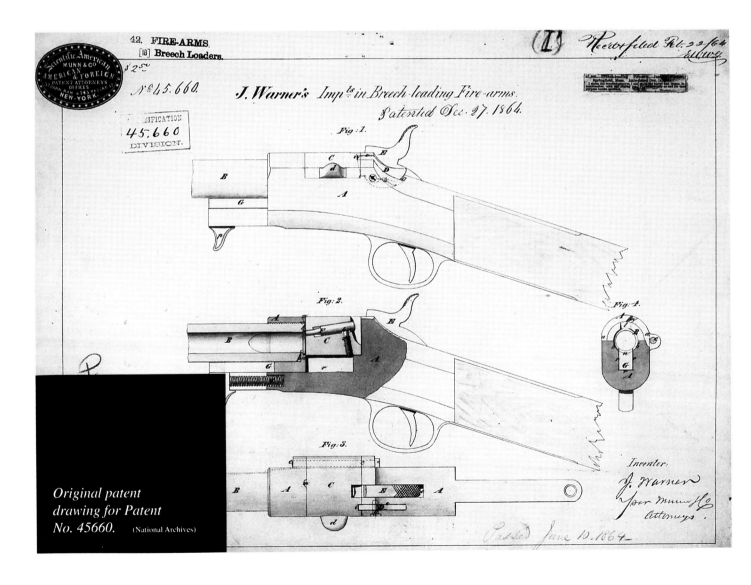

Original patent drawing for Patent No. 45660. (National Archives)

upper portion of the front of the lever and so presses it back until the block arises in the proper position when the lever is thrown into the notch by the spring.

The facility with which the breech block can be unlocked by merely shifting the thumb from the hammer to the locking lever simplifies the operation of reloading and enables the repetition of the fire to be performed very rapidly.

What I claim as my invention and desire to secure by Letters Patent is;

1st: the locking lever arranged in relation with the hammer and in combination with the movable breech piece to be operated upon and operate substantially as herein set forth.

2nd: The beveled grooves in the barrel and frame in combination with the sliding pin substantially as and for the purpose herein specified.

3rd: Providing a solid bearing directly under the cartridge shell extractor both while it is in position for firing and while it is being drawn back to extract the discharged shells from the barrel substantially as and for the purpose herein specified.

James Warner

More Problems with Washington

The patent office replied two months later with official approval of only one of Warner's three claims;[11]

James Warner
c/o Munn & Co.   April 21, 1864

Sir:

Your application for patent—Breech loading firearms has been examined. Your first claim is not seen to present any novelty; nothing being more common than for a movable chamber to be locked by a spring latch capable of being pressed open by the same thumb which is used to cock the hammer and without shifting the position of the hand. See the patents of R.S. Lawrence January 6, 1852 No 8637; of Henry Kellogg, May 20, 1862 No. 35,356 and Jackson and Goodrem March 17, 1863, No. 37,937. There is no novelty in supporting a sliding cartridge retractor throughout its entire movement; and it is moreover shown in the patent of J. Warner, February 23, 1864, No. 41,732. Your first and third claims must accordingly be rejected and your specifications and diagrams are herewith returned.

Respectfully,
William B. T.

Warner's attorneys quickly rewrote the application to remove claims 1 and 3 and resubmitted the amended application to the patent office on June 8th, 1864.[12] This resulted in patent No. 45,660 being issued to James Warner on December 27, 1864.[13]

It should be noted that both of Warner's breechloading patents deal with designs that were incorporated in both the Warner and Greene model arms and not specifically related to just one or the other model. The breechblock holding mechanism of patent No. 41,732 could however be argued to be a forerunner of that used in the Greene-manufactured Warner carbines.

The design of a spring-loaded firing pin in patent No. 41,732 had the additional benefit of being able to automatically withdraw the firing pin, should it accidentally penetrate the copper shell of the cartridge. This automatic withdrawal feature was not incorporated in his bevel design of patent No. 45,660. Obviously, Warner never appreciated the potential value of the feature and he eliminated the idea from both production models (one exception is known) in favor of his bevel system, as described in patent No. 45,660. In retrospect, this oversight would later become one of the major reasons for his weapon being withdrawn from the battlefield in the early part of 1865.

Beveled grooves on frame and rear of barrel, which cause firing pin to withdraw upon contact, are part of Patent No. 45660.   (Smithsonian Collection)

CHAPTER 2

WARNER FIREARMS

Warner Model Carbine

RECEIVER: Brass
CALIBER: .515
CARTRIDGE: .50 Warner rimfire and 56-56 Spencer rimfire
BARREL: 20 inches
GROOVES: 3
OVERALL: 37 1/2 inches
WEIGHT: 6 pounds, 12 ounces
PRODUCED: 1864-1865
NUMBER PRODUCED: 3,000
SERIAL NUMBER RANGE: 1-3000
COST: $18.00 (First contract)
        $20.00 (Second contract)
INSPECTORS MARKS: CSL
RECEIVER MARKINGS: James Warner, Springfield Mass
                     Warners
                     Patent

Warner model carbines were manufactured by James Warner at his own factory on the Pecousic Brook, just south of Springfield, Massachusetts. Barrels, bands, sling ring and bolt were finished in the white. The extractor, firing pin and all screws were fire-blued, while the hammer and trigger were case hardened. The two-piece black walnut stock was oil finished. Initials of Springfield Armory subinspector C. S. Leonard (CSL) will normally be found stamped on the left side of the barrel just ahead of the breech frame, above the forend and on the wrist of the buttstock on the left side, behind the breech frame.

The unmarked barrel is mounted with a clumsy looking, wide based front sight, 1/2 inch from the muzzle and a single leaf folding rear sight, graduated for 100, 300, 500 and 800 yards, located 2 1/4 inches forward of the frame. A single barrel band is held by a conventional spring beneath the stock. The forend is fastened to the barrel by a single screw.

The receiver, trigger guard and buttplate are made of brass. The split sling ring is carried on an eye bolt which passes through, and is secured by, a small, slotted, reverse-threaded nut, countersunk into the right side of the receiver. A plate with a small slot to facilitate removal is provided on the right side of the receiver to permit assembly and repair. A spring loaded manual cartridge extractor is located beneath the forward part of the receiver while a thumb lever located to the left of the centrally hung hammer serves as a breech securing device when the hammer is not fully forward.

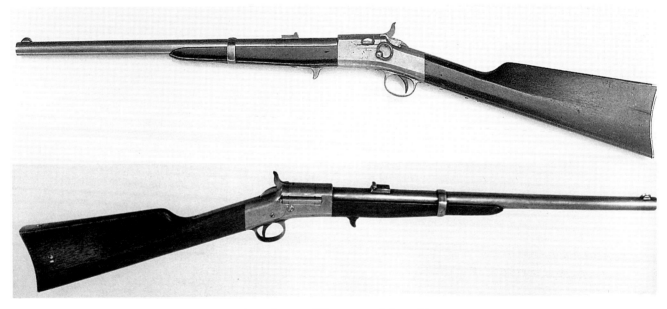

Standard production Warner model carbine.   (USMA Collection)

Detail of markings on the receiver of the standard Warner model (s/n 1666). Note CSL (Charles S. Leonard) inspector's mark on barrel. "CSL" appears on most Warner model carbines. Others bear only an "L". The vast number of arms with either stamp compared to those that lack any, indicate that carbines with either stamp were part of the 2801 guns delivered to the government.

(Smithsonian Collection)

Stock cartouche "CSL" found only on Warner model carbines.

(USMA Collection)

Warner model single leaf rear sight (above) and front sight (left)

(Author's Collection)

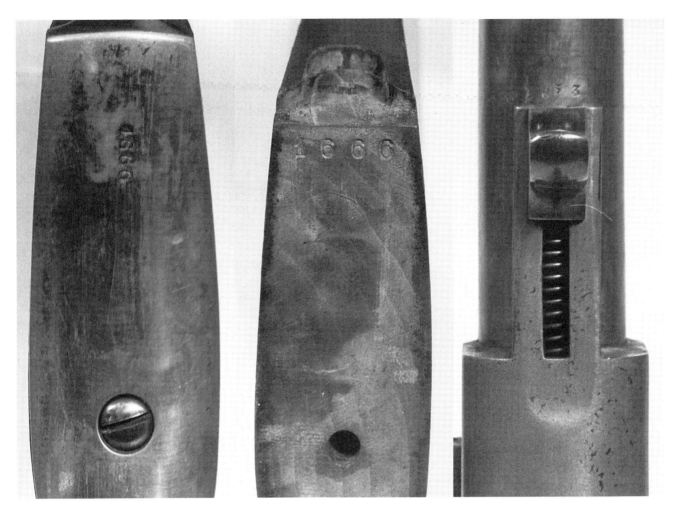

On Warner model carbines the serial number will be found on the butt plate, butt stock, underside of the barrel, and front flat of the receiver.   (Smithsonian Collection)

(Above) Warner model, right side detail. (Below) detail of receiver with side plate removed. (Smithsonian Collection)

A total of 2,801 Warner model carbines were purchased by the U.S. government. Of that number 1,001 were obtained at an individual cost of $18.00 under Warner's initial contract. An additional 500 arms were accepted in error. The price for these arms was later negotiated to be $20.00 each. All of these carbines were originally chambered for the .515 caliber Warner cartridge. Under a second contract, an additional 1,300 carbines, originally chambered for the 56-56 Spencer rimfire cartridge, were delivered, at a cost of $20.00 each.

During the period from November 1864 to January 1865, an estimated 500 of the first 1,501 Warner model carbines were rechambered for the 56-56 Spencer cartridge by U.S. Ordnance personnel at the Washington, D.C., Arsenal.

Evidence suggests that 450 Warner model carbines chambered for the Warner cartridge were initially issued to Companies C and E of the 1st Wisconsin Volunteer Cavalry. They were used by this unit between August 1864 and March 1865. The 500 carbines rechambered for the 56-56 Spencer cartridge at the Washington Arsenal were issued to companies A through I of the 3rd Massachusetts Volunteer Cavalry Regiment in January 1865.

There is no evidence that any of the 1,300 Warner model carbines delivered under the second contract were ever issued to Federal cavalry units. Records of postwar surplus arms sales suggest that the entire second contract lot of 2,500 carbines was sold and shipped to France in 1870, in anticipation of the Franco-Prussian War.

Greene Model Warner Carbine

RECEIVER: Brass
CALIBER: .515
CARTRIDGE: 56-56 Spencer rimfire or 56-50 Spencer rimfire
BARREL: 20 inches
GROOVES: 3
OVERALL: 37 1/2 inches
WEIGHT: 6 pounds 12 ounces
PRODUCED: 1864-1865
NUMBER PRODUCED: 3,000
SERIAL NUMBER RANGE: 1-3000
COST: $20.00
INSPECTORS MARKS: CDR or MM
RECEIVER MARKINGS: Greene Rifle Works
Worcester, Mass.
Pat'd 1864

Greene model carbines were manufactured under contract to James Warner by the Greene Rifle Works at their facilities in the Junction Shop at Worcester, Massachusetts. Barrel, barrel band, extractor, firing pin, screws, sling ring and bar were finished either in the white or blued. Hammer and trigger were case hardened. The two piece black walnut stock was oil finished. Initials of Springfield Armory subinspector Maurice Moulton (MM), or those of an unidentified inspector (CDR), will occasionally be found stamped on the left side of the receiver just behind the barrel, and on the buttplate in back of the top screw. None have been observed on the wrist of the buttstock.

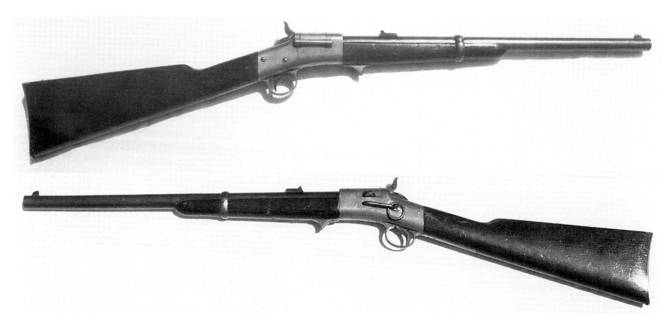

Standard production Greene model carbine.   (Author's Collection)

Standard production Greene model receiver markings.   (Author's Collection)

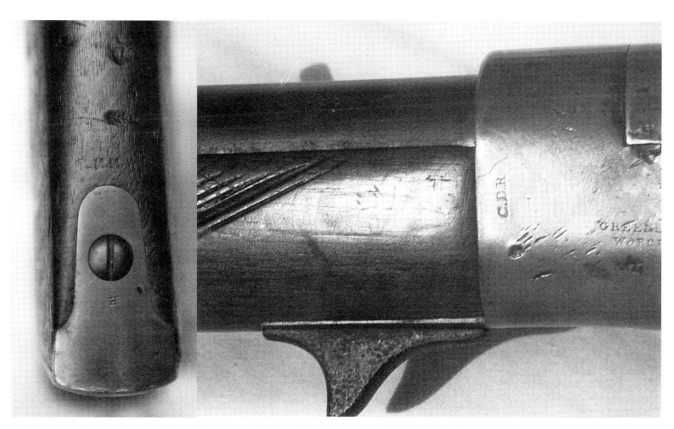

Inspector's marks noted on Greene model carbines consist of "MM" for inspector Maurice Moulton and "CDR" of an unknown inspector.

(Author's Collection)

The unmarked barrel is mounted with a wide based front sight, 1/2 inch from the muzzle, and a single-leaf folding rear sight, graduated for 100, 300, 500 and 800 yards, located 2 1/4 inches forward of the frame. A single barrel band is held by a conventional spring beneath the stock. The forestock is fastened to the barrel by a single screw.

The receiver, trigger guard and buttplate are made of brass. The solid sling ring is carried on a conventional style 1 3/4 inch bar mounted on the left side of the receiver. A plate without a slot to facilitate removal is provided on the right side of the receiver to permit assembly and repair. A spring-loaded cartridge extractor is located beneath the forward part of the receiver. A knurled button on the left side of the breechblock actuates a spring-loaded plunger and serves as a breech securing device when the hammer is not fully forward.

A total of 1,200 Greene model carbines were purchased by the U.S. government at a cost of $20.00 each under James Warner's second contract. All carbines provided by the Greene Rifle Works under this government contract were chambered for the 56-56 Spencer rimfire cartridge.

There is no indication that any of the Greene model arms ever were issued to U.S. Cavalry units. Records of postwar surplus arms sales suggest the entire second contract lot of 2,500 carbines were sold and shipped to France in 1870.

An unknown number of Greene model Warner rifles were also produced. The rifle is similar in all respects to the standard production Greene model carbine, except for an improved breechblock securing mechanism, 28 inch barrel, high quality stock finish, and lack of a saddle ring bar. A carbine model, similar in all respects to the rifle except for barrel length and an unconventional bolt mounting a split saddle ring has also been noted. As will be found with all Greene produced weapons above serial number 2300, both weapons observed were chambered for the 56-50 Spencer rimfire cartridge. Examination of the one rifle and one carbine indicated both were made at the end of the production run, possibly for the civilian market.

Top view of a Greene model receiver showing gas vent hole and extractor pulled halfway back. Serial numbers for Greene model arms will be found on the receiver (shown), breech block, trigger guard, cover plate, extractor, breech block release button and barrel.

(Author's Collection)

Comparison of Greene model carbine sights.

(Left) Standard model front sight.
(Center) Standard model single leaf rear sight.
(Right) Early model rear sight lacking range marks and has oval shaped range apertures. (Springfield Armory Museum Collection)

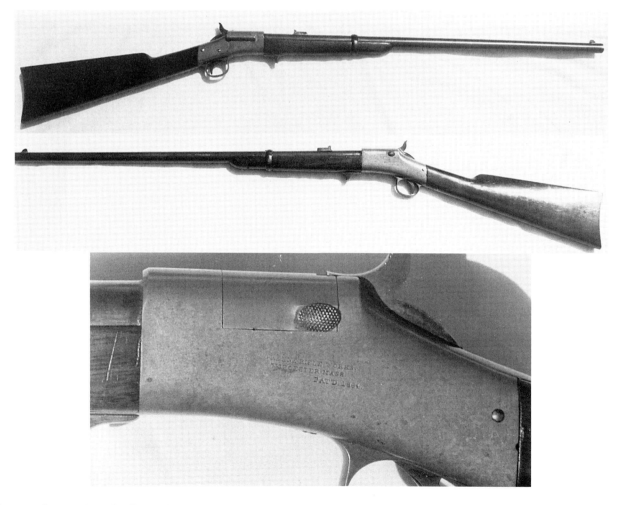

Greene also produced rifles. These differed from the carbines only in the length of the barrel and the lack of a sling ring and bar. Note the improved, flush-mounted breech block release button found on later models. (Author's Collection)

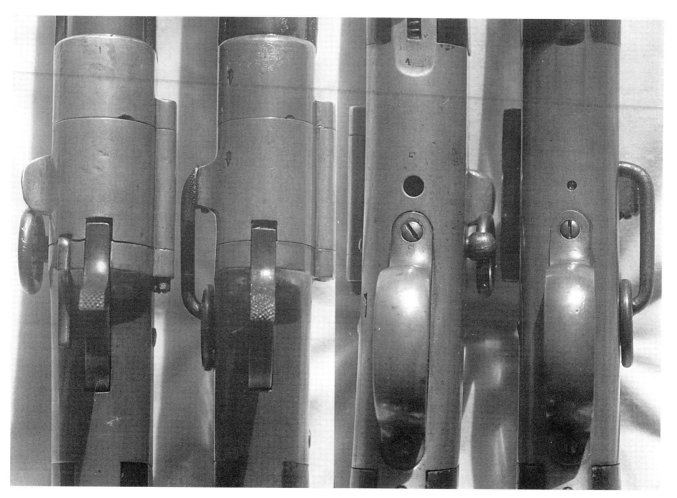

Receiver, top view. Warner model (left) and
Greene model (right). (Author's Collection)

Receiver, bottom view. Warner model (left) and
Greene model (right). (Author's Collection)

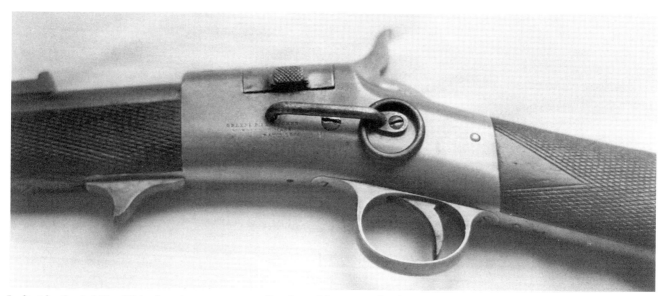

Left side, Serial No. 294, showing cap screw. Stock and forearm checkerings are believed to be post-war additions
by surplus arms brokers to enhance sales on the civilian market.

(Author's Collection)

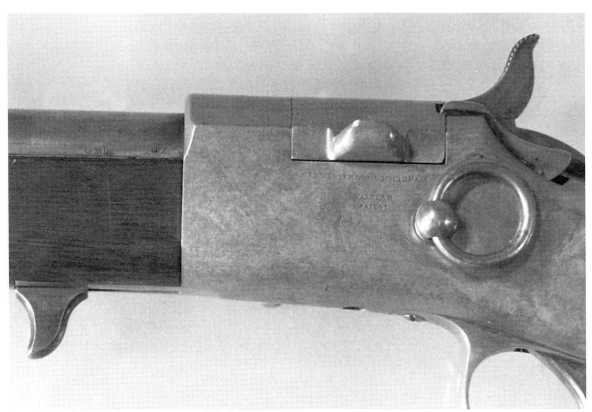

Comparison of breech block thumb release levers. (Above) original style of thumb release as found on Warner models. (Below) the thumb release on early Greene models was scored but otherwise contoured much like Warner model arms.

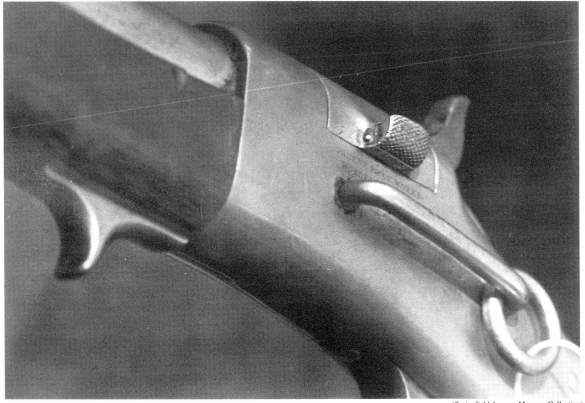

Comparison of breech blocks and thumb release buttons on Greene models. (Above) standard thumb release and breech block. (Below) the flush mounted thumb release found on later models.

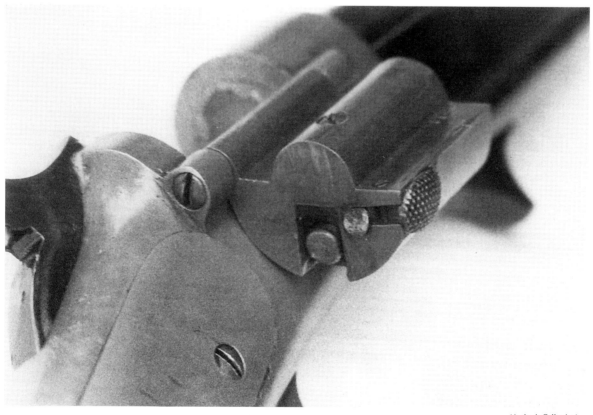

CHAPTER 3

GOVERNMENT CONTRACTS

The First Carbine Contract

On February 24, 1863 James Warner submitted his first patent application for a breechloading firearm. Despite the fact that he had not been granted a patent, he approached the Ordnance Office on March 27th and proposed to furnish "20,000 Patent Breech Loading Carbines at twenty-two dollars each". The sample carbine he provided was examined by Captain Treadwell who returned it to Warner with a report of his evaluation. Although there might have been problems with the arm, it was regarded as suitable enough for service for the War Department:[1]

Messers Jas Warner & Co.   Ordnance Office
Springfield, Mass.   Washington - April 27, 1863

Gentlemen:

On your proposal of the 27th inst the War department has directed that a contract be made for one thousand of your carbines according to a model to be approved by this office, with the understanding that, if the arms on delivery prove to be well made and adapted to the service, then all that the contractor can manufacture to the end of 1863 will be received. With a view to you presenting a model to be approved here, I have requested Major Hagner, Inspector of Contract Arms, to examine your arm when you present it to him for that purpose, and to report to this office what changes and modifications, if any it requires to make it a suitable and effective arm for the military service. When the model is approved, a contract will be sent to you.

Respectfully,
Jas W. Ripley
Br. Genl. Chief Ord.

Shortly thereafter Warner was sent a contract for his first government order. However, even though the in-structions in General Ripley's cover letter were specific, the bureaucratic exactitudes would later obviously cause Warner a good deal of frustration:[2]

Messers Jas Warner & CO.   Ordnance Office
Springfield Mass.   Washington - May 8, 1863.

Gentlemen

Your offer to the Secretary of War to furnish Warner Breech Loading Carbines (having certain modifications) has been approved, I transmit herewith quadruplicate copies of a contract and bond which you will be pleased to execute and return to this office.

I would also call your attention to the Act approved July 1, 1862 entitled the Act to Provide Internal Revenue which requires that stamps shall be attached to all contracts — which in this case will be one of the value of 5 cents for each copy of the contract and one of the value of 10 cents for each certificate on each copy making in all 4 of the value of 5 cents each (of three certificates on each copy) 12 of the value of 10 cents each, and also requires, that when executed, the stamps shall be canceled.

Respectfully
Jas W. Ripley
Br. Genl. Chief Ord.

On May 21st, Ripley received a letter from Warner stating that the copy of the contract was not in accordance with his understanding of the instructions from the Secretary of War. In short, he expected to receive a contract for a great deal more than just one thousand arms. Ripley attempted to justify the governments position in his response:[3]

Brigadier General James W. Ripley. (USAMHI)

Messers Warner & Co.   Ordnance
Springfield, Mass.   Washington - May 22, 1863

Gentlemen

Your letter of the 19th inst. in relation to your contract for one thousand carbines is received. The contract sent to you for execution, was drawn under the following instructions of the War Department endorser. Your proposal to manufacture breech loading carbines dated April 27, 1863 was referred to the Chief of Ordnance with instructions to enter into a contract for one thousand of these arms according to a model arm to be approved by him with the understanding that if the arms on delivery prove to be well made and adapted to the service, then all that the contractor can manufacture "to 31 December 1863 will be received." When the condition on which the above understanding is based shall have been fulfilled it will be carried into effect, but it is not a part of the contract for the 1000 arms. As regards appendages, they are always included in contracts for arms; the price uniformly embracing them with the arms which are not fit for service without them.

Your proposal specified that the first thousand arms were to be delivered in July next.

Respectfully
Jas W. Ripley
Br. Gen'l. Chf. Ord.

Warner accepted this explanation, but his problems were only beginning. Following receipt of Captain Treadwell's list of recommended changes in early April, Warner had been working on an improved model. This was apparently accomplished in June 1863, and the model was resubmitted for approval. Although Major Hagner, Inspector of Contract Arms in New York, approved the model, it still needed refinement. These changes to his carbine required continuous retooling and thus further delayed full scale production. This concerned Warner enough to explain the problem to Ripley:[4]

General James W. Ripley   Chief of Ordnance
Springfield, Mass.   Washington DC - July 6, 1863

Dear Sir

We have perfected a model carbine on Friday last and submitted it to Major Hagner, who approved it. The alterations suggested by him under your order, "to make it an efficient arm" have most unexpectedly delayed us involving the making of some new tools and the alterations of those already made. We shall not therefore be able to make deliveries until the last of this or first part of next month. We are very truly yours

James Warner & Co.

Warner's production problems must have been greater than he had anticipated, for by late October he still had not made his initial arms delivery. In a possible effort to circumvent the requirement to provide the government with an "approved" model prior to any delivery of weapons, he wrote to the Honorable P.H. Watson in hope that he could influence the Ordnance Department. However, from the tone of General Ramsay's October 29th letter, it is clear that the contract would be followed to the letter:[5]

Messers Jas Warner & Co.   Ordnance Office
Springfield, Mass.   Washington - Oct. 27, 1863

Gentlemen

Your letter of the 21st inst. to the Hon. P.H. Watson has been referred to this office. You may recollect that on 28 April 1863, the Secretary of War directed that a contract should be made with you for a thousand carbines on "Certain Terms" according to a model and approved by the Chief of Ordnance.

This Department is fully aware of the history of this model and of Col. Hagner's connection with it - but until the model is sent here and approved by the "Chief of Ordnance" the contract cannot be consummated.

On the 25th inst. Col. Hagner was directed to send an inspector to your factory to take up and inspect what work was ready with a view of facilitating the delivery of the carbines when the order or contract was made. He was also directed to send two approved models to this office, one to be retained here as a standard, the other to be used by Col. Hagner as a model, in inspecting the work.

As soon as these models are received prompt action will be taken and the orders of the War Department carried out.

Respectfully
Geo D. Ramsay
Br. Gen'l. Ch. Ord.

Brigadier General George D. Ramsay. (USAMHI)

Warner was running out of time. He had yet to supply the Ordnance Office with an acceptable carbine that could serve as a model. Until that was accomplished the government would not accept any of his guns. To make matters worse, the part of his contract permitting him to supply as many carbines as he could produce was scheduled to expire at the end of the year. In mid-December 1863 he made still another attempt of submitting two model carbines that would be acceptable to the Ordnance Office. However, the samples he provided were again rejected:[6]

Office of Inspector of Contract Arms
No. 77 East 14th Street
New York - November 16, 1863

General G.D. Ramsay
Chief of Ordnance
Washington

General

Mr. Warner has sent to me two of his carbines — one of which with 100 cartridges, 1 screw driver and 1 wiper and thong I sent to you by express. Mr. Warner has not fully carried out my recommendations as reported to the Ord. Office May 5th, 1863.

1st. The swivel ring bolt should have a thread under the head, of different size from that on the end, and screwing into the nut, so that the bolt could not unscrew until the nut was removed. At present this bolt might unscrew by ordinary use and the nut might be lost.

2nd. The screw driver is inferior in quality to the one recommended and should be so made as to serve the purpose of a spring vice in taking out and putting in the main spring.

Some provisions will be necessary for removing the movable lock cover without battering the edges. It is now likely to be marred and cannot then be replaced without filing.

The band will have to be secured by a spring I think, as there is very little spare space to take up by the screw, and exposure will probably soon loosen the band enough to make it slip when the gun is fired. There being but one band it is the more important to preserve this.

Very respectfully yours
Your obedient servant
P.V. Hagner
Lt. Col. Ordnance Inspector

By late December, with virtually no time remaining on his contract, Warner apparently resorted to attempt a bluff in order to deliver at least one hundred carbines. However Hagner would have nothing to do with it and wrote Ramsay regarding the situation:[7]

Office of Inspector of Contract Arms
No. 77 East 14th Street
New York - December 28th, 1863

General G.D. Ramsay
Chief of Ordnance
Washington

General

Mr. Warner reports that he will have ready to ship on Thursday to you the sample carbine corrected as required by me. He says that he had verbal directions to send the first 100 guns he could get ready as soon as possible and he hopes to have the 100 in a week.

Please instruct me.

1st — Whether I am to receive these carbines and what number.

2nd — Where they are to be sent and in what lots.

3rd — Price to be paid for them.

No definite order has been sent to me regarding the receipt of this carbine.

I have no orders yet about the Lindsay Double Musket and have not yet sent an inspector there.

Very respectfully
P.V. Hagner
Lt. Col. Ordnance

On December 31st, 1863, Warner again forwarded a model carbine to the Ordnance Office. This gun was serial number 94 and from all indications, complied with all the required improvements previously set forth by Capt. Treadwell and Lt. Col. Hagner.[8]

Colonel William A. Thornton replaced Lt. Colonel Hagner as Inspector of Small Arms on January 1, 1864. Accordingly, General Ramsay restated the government's position regarding receipt of any of Warner's carbines prior to receipt of an acceptable model:[9]

Col. W.A. Thornton   Ordnance Office
Inspector of Small Arms   War Department
                 Washington - Jan. 2, 1864
Sir

I have to acknowledge receipt of a letter from Lt. Col. Hagner dated Dec. 28 stating that Mr. Warner had informed him that he was going to forward 100 carbines to him and asking whether he was to receive these carbines and what number etc. I have to inform you that no carbines are to be received from Mr. Warner, he having no authority to deliver any. By direction of the Secretary of War a contract for 1,000 is to be given him when he forwards a model carbine approved by the Chief of Ordnance — which has not yet been done.

Respectfully
Gen. D. Ramsay
Br. Gen'l. Ch. of Ord.

With the model carbine finally approved, Ramsay indicated that the contract of one thousand arms would be promptly forwarded. However he also pointed out that Warner was required to provide two model guns:[10]

Jas Warner   Ordnance Office
Springfield, Mass.   Washington - Jan. 7, 1864

Sir

Your letter of the 30th transmitting a carbine and appendages has been received. The carbine has been approved and sent to Col. Thornton. You must forward another of the same pattern to be kept at this office. The contract for one thousand (1000) at $18.00 each will be made out and sent to you tomorrow.

                              Respectfully
                              Geo D. Ramsay
                              Br. Gen'l. Chf. Ord.

Ramsay then informed Thornton that the sample carbine had been forwarded to be used as a model for inspection of the guns to be delivered under his one thousand gun contract:[11]

Col. W.A. Thornton   Ordnance Office
77 East 14th Street N.Y.   War Department
                        Washington, DC - Jan. 7, 1864

Sir

I have this day sent you by Express a "Warner Carbine" and appendages, which carbine will serve as a model for those to be delivered by him under a contract to be made out in a few days. When this contract shall have been duly executed and approved a copy will be sent you.

                              Respectfully
                              Geo D. Ramsay
                              Br. Gen'l. Ch. of Ord.

Although Warner mailed his sample carbine (S.N.94) to Ramsay on December 31st, Thornton wrote Warner on January 6th and said he had not yet received it. This obviously concerned Warner enough to reply directly to Ramsay on January 8th, 1864:[12]

Br. Gen. G.D. Ramsay   Chief of Ordnance
Springfield, Mass.   Washington - Jan. 8, 1864

Sir

I am informed by letter dated January 6 from Col. W. A. Thornton that you were not in receipt of a model carbine, from me up to January 5th.

December 31st, 1863 I sent you one gun per Express, modified in accordance to instructions received from Col. P.V. Hagner by letter of Nov. 20th.

                              I Remain
                              Your Obedient Servant
                              Jas Warner

On January 11th, Ramsay forwarded the contract for one thousand carbines. Warner had failed to meet the original contract offer to provide "one thousand carbines of the model approved, and if they were found suitable for service, then all that can be manufactured to the end of 1863." Since that part of the contract could no longer be met the new contract was changed to require the purchase of only one thousand carbines with a delivery date on or before May 1st, 1864:[13]

James Warner Esq.   Ordnance Office
Springfield, Mass.   January 11th, 1864

Sir

I transmit herewith quadruplicate copies of a contract for 1,000 carbines which you will be pleased to execute and immediately return.

The certificate as to ability of sureties must be signed by a Judge of a court of the U.S.

                              Geo D. Ramsay
                              Br. Gen'l. Ch. of Ord.

Warner was anxious to begin deliveries and promptly returned the contract with the required signatures but Ramsay returned it stating it had been incorrectly accomplished:[14]

James Warner Esq.   Ordnance Office
Springfield, Mass.   January 20th, 1864

Sir

I return herewith the "duplicate", "triplicate" and "quadruplicate" copies of your contract for 1,000 Warner carbines, that the certificate as to the ability of the sureties may be signed by a Judge of the U.S. Court, as required by the Secretary of War. Until that is done, the contract cannot be completed by my signature, nor can it be completed until the five copies of the contract are returned.

                              Geo D. Ramsay
                              Br. Gen'l. Ch. of Ord.

On January 25th Warner replied to Ramsay's letter telling him that, in fact, he had completed the contract correctly. However, on February 5th the contract was again returned to Warner for his failure to attach the required number of U.S. Revenue stamps.

By this time Warner had to have been impatient and was unaware that his contract was being returned. On February 8th, he again wrote Ramsay expressing his concern that the contract was returned "some three weeks since" and may have become lost in the mail. Apparently, he received the contract that same day, for on February 9th he wrote that he had returned the contract with the appropriate revenue stamps attached.

On February 15th Ramsay sent him the good news:[15]

James Warner Esq.   Ordnance Office
Springfield, Mass.   February 15, 1864

Sir

     Your contract for 1,000 carbines has been completed by my signature and approved by the Secretary of War. I enclose a copy for your use.

                              Geo D. Ramsay
                              Br. Gen'l. Ch. of Ord.

Production Begins

This new contract put Warner on the spot. It required him to deliver the one thousand arms on or before May, 1st, 1864. If his past ability to provide a satisfactory model was any measure of his current production capability, he was in real trouble. On February 27th, he wrote to Ramsay addressing this very problem. Additionally he made the first mention of his subcontract with the Greene Rifle Works in Worcester Massachusetts, to assist him in the manufacture of his carbine:[16]

                         Br. Gen. Geo D. Ramsay
                         Chief of Ordnance
                    Washington DC - Feb. 27, 1864
Sir

     About the first of May 1863, I presented to the Ordnance Department a sample of a carbine called "Warner" Carbine and received an order for one thousand of the same with liberty to produce all I could until December 31, 1863.

     This order was conditional, that your Department was at liberty to suggest such alterations and improvements as would make the "arm" more efficient and serviceable.

     Under this last clause the sample was turned over to Major Hagner, to direct what alterations and improvements should be made. So much time was contained in complying with his suggestions and requirements that no carbines were completed within the time specified, and a new contract or order was made, extending the time until the first of May next.

     In order to increase the production of the "arm" on the first day of October last I made a contract with the "Greene Rifle Works" to manufacture my carbine. That company at once commenced the manufacture of the "Arm" at their works in Worcester, Massachusetts. The company is now ready for the services of an inspector, and will be able to make deliveries during the month of March and desire that one be sent immediately to Worcester, to inspect the work.

                         Respectfully yours
                         James Warner
                         by John L. King

By February 27th, it was apparent to the Ordnance Department that Warner was not going to provide a second model carbine, even though they had reminded him of this requirement on January 7th. To solve the problem, they ordered Thornton to forward a carbine that had passed inspection to serve as their model:[17]

Col. W.A. Thornton   Ordnance Office
Inspector of Small Arms   War Department
                    Washington, DC - Feb. 27, 1864
Sir

     On the 7th of January there was sent you from this office, by Express, one sample Warners carbine and appendages, to serve as a model for those to be delivered under a contract, then about to be executed. As it is reported that you have no sample carbine to inspect by, you will please state for the information of this Department whether the Carbine was received by you.

     You will please forward to this office one of the Warner Carbines that shall have passed inspection as a model to be deposited here.

                    By order — Geo T. Balch Capt. Ord.
                              Prin. Asst. Ch. of Ord.

On February 28, Warner again wrote to Ramsay requesting an inspector be sent to Worcester to proof the arms being made by the Greene Rifle Works. Obviously Warner's intent was to get his foot in the door by getting the arms inspected. Once passed, he assumed sale to the government would be that much easier:[18]

                         Br. Gen. Geo D. Ramsay
                         Chief of Ordnance
                    Washington, DC - Feb. 29, 1864
Dear Sir:

     We ask that you will direct Colonel Thornton to send an inspector to inspect the carbines being made for me at Worcester Mass by the Greene Rifle Co.

     I do not claim that the government is bound to receive these arms when completed but if the government should find it for its interest to buy the arms when completed, as I have no doubt it will, much time and expense will be saved both to the government and to the parties interested.

                         James Warner
                         by John L. King

Apparently Ramsay must have thought Warner had a good idea, for he promptly accepted Warner's offer and issued Thornton instructions to that effect. It is interesting to note that the order instructing Thornton to send an inspector to the Greene Works contains the first mention of the number of carbines (i.e. 3,000) that were being produced there:[19]

Mr. James Warner　　　　　　　Ordnance Office
Springfield, Mass.　　　　　　　　War Department
　　　　　　Washington, DC - Mar. 1, 1864
Sir:

Your letter of the 29th February from Mr. John L. King in relation to having a U.S. Inspector sent to the Greene Rifle Works at Worcester, Mass. to pass upon the work on Warners Carbine now in progress there is received.

On the conditions specified in your letter namely that you do not claim that the Government is bound to receive these arms when completed, on account of this act I have today directed Col. Thornton to detail an inspector to go to Worcester for the purpose indicated:

By order Geo T. Balch
Capt. of Ord. Prin. Asst. to
Chief of Ord.

Col. W. A. Thornton　　　　　　Ordnance Office
Inspector of Contract Arms　　　War Department
77 East Fourteenth St., NY　　　Washington, DC
　　　　　　　　　　　　　　　　Mar. 1, 1864
Sir:

You will please detail a competent subinspector to go to the Greene Rifle Works at Worcester, Mass. to inspect (but not to receive) such work on the Warner carbines, say 3000, as they have now in progress which the company may present to him.

This order is not to involve any obligation whatever to receive these arms at any future time as you will perceive by a copy of a letter to Mr. Warner herein enclosed, but merely that in case the Government should find it for its interest to buy the arms when completed, time and expense may be saved both the Government and the parties.

Respectfully,
Your Obedient Servant
By order Geo T. Balch
Capt. of Ord. Prin. Asst. to
Chief of Ord.

Little more than a week later Thornton gave a good picture of the situation at the Greene Works. He clearly indicated that not only was the Greene operation not an industrial giant, but that a shortage of ammunition was also holding up the final proof of any assembled arms:[20]

Office of Inspector of Contract Arms
No. 77 East 14th Street
New York - March 8th, 1864
Brig Gen. G.D. Ramsay
Chief of Ordnance
Washington D.C.

General

I have received your communication of the 1st inst. and have the honor to inform you that I have detailed a competent SubInspector to inspect (but not to receive) component parts for Warners Carbine at the Greene Rifle Works, Worcester, Mass. He reports there is not more than two or three days work for one man in the inspection of parts. There are about 1500 arms ready for proof which he will commence when he gets the ammunition.

W. A. Thornton
Col. Ordnance Inspector

Despite this, the sub-inspector apparently remained at Worcester. Thornton honored Ramsays request for a second model carbine on March 19th by sending him carbine, serial number 1666. Additionally he provided some opinion on the faults of the arm:[21]

Office of the Inspector of Contract Arms
Washington, DC - Mar. 19, 1864
General G. D. Ramsay
Chief of Ordnance

Sir

I have the honor to report that I have inspected one of James Warners Carbines No. 1666 which pursuant to your instructions of Oct 29, ultimo is forwarded as a sample of the carbines now being furnished by him pursuant to contracts.

In my opinion, the application of the stock tip to the barrel by a screw is a bad adjustment: for the reason that the tapping for the screw is some times deep, and if the screw is also long, the driving of the screw home will raise a perfection in the bore by the point of the screw. In the formation of the barrel a stud should be left or a stud should be brazed on for the

"Pattern Model" Warner model carbine, Serial No. 1666.　　　(Smithsonian Collection)

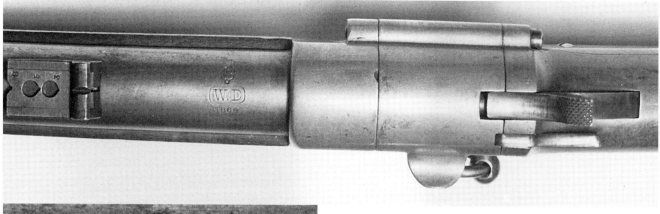

Top view of carbine, Serial No. 1666, clearly showing placement of War Department stamp denoting a "Pattern Model" arm. (Smithsonian Collection)

reception of the stock tip screw. Either would be better than the present arrangement which is found to act badly in adjusting the rear sight base in the like manner to the musket barrel. The screw is also very large, in fact much greater than is needful for the assemblage of the tip to the barrel.

The screws for the Guard Plate should be duplicated and not of unequal lengths, nor so long as to prevent the bending of the sear spring, as will be found to be the case if the front screw is applied in the rear screw orifice.

It is presumed that if the main and sear spring were combined in one that a better spring would be produced. In any case the sear spring should have a longer bearing in rear of the screw hole.

The milling under the guard plate is roughly done. The rear sight is roughly finished and consequently the bluing is bad. The front sight is large and clumsey in appearance. The finish of the sear nose is in three of four bevels and consequently imperfect. Still I consider the carbine I herewith furnish, a better arm than No. 94 set to me on the 9th of January as a model.

I consider it proper here to remark that improvement to the Warner Carbine is being made by the Greene Rifle Works at Worcester Mass, which in the end I think will be of great advantage to the arms.

W. A. Thornton
Col. of Ord.

Of Thorntons numerous suggestions for improvement, only duplicating the length of both trigger guard screws, refining the milling under the trigger guard, and improving the finish of the rear sight were ever eventually changed. It is interesting to note his comment that he regarded the Greene arm to be an "improvement" over the model produced by Warner in his works at Springfield.

By the positive tone of Warner's April 5th letter it appeared that the situation had changed in that ammunition was readily available and carbine production was progressing well:[22]

Br. Gen. Geo D. Ramsay   Springfield Mass.
Chief of Ordnance   April 5, 1864
Washington, DC

Sir:

I forwarded March 31st two hundred (200) of my carbines to Lt. Col. R. A. Wainwright by order of Col. W. A. Thornton.

In a few days shall send two hundred (200) more. I have the ammunition suitable for the above carbines so that they can be put to trial and use at once if desired. Shall I forward it and if so where?

Jas Warner

However, Colonel Thornton was sufficiently concerned about the progress Warner was making to telegraph General Ramsay on April 8th, stating that as of that date "only two hundred Warner carbines have been inspected and received." With only three weeks remaining on this contract Thornton apparently suspected that Warner was in danger of defaulting.[23]

Warner's April 5th offer to provide ammunition (probably for the limited number of weapons already furnished) was interpreted by Ramsay to be an offer for an unlimited amount. Accordingly, he asked Warner to state his price and furnish a sample. Warner apparently took advantage of his good fortune and offered to supply 500,000 rounds at $25 per thousand. The government quickly accepted the offer and stated a contract would be forwarded the following day. Additionally, they were anxious to receive a delivery date and on April 25th instructed Warner to reply by telegraph.[24]

Problems with Deliveries

By April 23rd Warner had only delivered five hundred carbines. To complicate the situation, Major Alexander B. Dyer, Commander of the Springfield Armory, had found a problem with Warners carbine during a test he conducted on April 16th, and reported this to the Ordnance Office. The problem stemmed from lack of a method to release pressure within the breech frame should the firing pin penetrate the cartridge. Warner's solution was to simply drill a vent hole vertically through the breech frame. Further tests appeared to confirm its effectiveness. On April 22nd Ramsay instructed Thornton to review Dyer's findings and, if he approved, have them carried out.[25] Under the understanding that this modification "would materially improve the arm without adding to the price" Thornton accepted and paid for the first five hundred carbines on April 25th, 1864.

Warner must have realized that time was running out and that he was not going to be able to deliver the remaining five hundred carbines by May 1st. On April 27th he made an unexpected proposal by offering to supply the 10,000 cartridges he had on hand at $26 per thousand and 50,000 carbines, in addition to requesting an extension of forty days to his current contract.[26] Ramsay responded to Warner's proposal on April 29th with two letters:[27]

James Warner Esq.   Ordnance Office
Springfield, Mass.   April 29, 1864

Sir:

Your letter of the 27th inst. regarding Warner's carbine and cartridges for it has been received. An order has been sent you this day for the 10,000 cartridges you had on hand.

You will please make for the information of this office at the earliest possible moment your acceptance or non-acceptance of the contract for 500,000 cartridges at $25 offered you. It is perhaps for your interest to make the cartridges, as the success of the carbine will necessarily depend greatly upon the

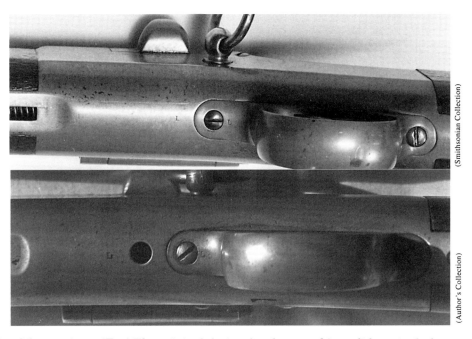

The underside of the receiver. (Top) The original design for these carbines did not include a gas vent hole. (Bottom) As a result of testing, the receivers were later modified to incorporate this safety feature.

manner in which the cartridges are manufactured, and should you manufacture them it would be for you interest to furnish the best possible ones.

Regarding your proposition to enter into a contract for 50,000 of your carbines (no price stated) I have to inform you that no action can be taken in the matter until the 1,000 now due under your contract shall have been tried in service and the reports regarding them received.

Geo D. Ramsay
Br. Gen. Ch. of Ord.

James Warner Esq.   Ordnance Office
Springfield, Mass.   April 29, 1864
Sir:

Be pleased to furnish for the use of this Department and deliver at the New York Agency No. 45, Worth Street, New York, ten thousand (10,000) primed Metallic Cartridges for the Warner Carbine. They are to be subject to the usual inspection and are to be delivered on or before the 20th day of May 1864. You will be paid at the rate of twenty five dollars ($25) per thousand upon the usual certificates of inspection and receipt, in such funds as the Treasury Department may provide. They are to be packaged as the inspector may direct.

Geo D. Ramsay
Br. Gen. Ch. of Ord.

Apparently Ramsay considered one offer to supply cartridges at $25 per thousand to be good for all offers. On the following day, as a result of not having delivered all 1,000 carbines by May 1st, 1864, Warner's contract automatically expired. Accordingly, on that date Colonel Thornton informed General Ramsay of his actions:[28]

Office of Inspector of Contract Arms
240 Broadway
New York - May 5th, 1864
Br. Gen. G. D. Ramsay
Chief of Ordnance
Washington

General:
I have the honor to inform you that I have closed the inspection of Warner Carbines, because of the expiration of his contract to deliver 1,000 on or before the first day of May 1864.

W. A. Thornton
Ordnance Inspector

Receiving notification that the inspector at Springfield would be withdrawn, and having heard nothing in regard to his request for an extension to his contract,

Warner quickly wrote Ramsay explaining the situation and requested that his inspector be permitted to remain:[29]

Springfield Arms Company
Br. Gen. Geo D. Ramsay   May 6, 1864
Dear Sir:

I beg to call attention to my letter under date April 27th in reference to my request for an extension of time in my contract with the U.S. Government for delivery of the remaining portion of the 1,000 of my breech loading carbines. I therein stated the delays I have been subjected to from various modifications suggested by authority, during the progress of their manufacture has retarded the fulfillment of the contract by the 1st inst. as provided. As an instance imposed, there is a modification recently suggested by Major Dyer of to which I drew your attention for reply in my letter of the 27 ultimo, and I shall be happy if it meets approval to carry it out. The remaining portion of the carbines, viz 500, are in a nearly finished state, and in my letter I requested 40 days extension for their completion and delivery.

The Government Inspector at my works, Mr. Leonard, has today received a notice from Col. Thornton for his removal, supposing my contract to be completed. I trust under the circumstances you will grant me the extension applied for, and the continuance of the inspector during completion.

James Warner

The effect that war was having on the factories of New England was two fold. Manufacturers were saturated with government orders, but draft quotas were drawing off both experienced and inexperienced workers who were needed to complete those contracts. Warners decision to decline the contract for a half million cartridges was most probably due in part to those situations. Despite this, Warner was still willing to sell what apparently was his entire stock of cartridges, retaining only enough to proof his carbines:[30]

Springfield Arms Company, Mass.
May 7, 1864
Brig. Gen'l. Geo D. Ramsay
Chief Ordnance
War Department

Dear Sir:
Referring to your letter of the 29th April I have forwarded this day to Capt. S. Crispin all the cartridges I had on hand (reserved for my own use in proving my carbines) viz nine boxes counting nine thousand cartridges.

I find I must decline the contract for 500,000 cartridges offered. The reason for doing so, which I regret, being that the cartridge markers in this and numerous other localities to which my inquiries have extended, are so full of contracts and orders that they cannot name any time as to the completion of a contract, nor will they name a definite price in the future at which they would take one from the constant increase in price of the materials. To avoid these difficulties in future I am erecting machinery and works for the manufacture of cartridges suitable to my carbines and shall give you timely intimation of my ability to enter into any contracts for a supply.

James Warner

Warners bid for a contract extension was successful. On May 10th General Ramsay instructed Colonel Thornton to return whatever carbines he had already accepted to Warner's Springfield works for modification. In addition, he informed Warner that his contract had been extended until June 10th, 1864:[31]

Col. W. A. Thornton   Ordnance Office
Inspector of Small Arms   War Department
                               Washington, DC
                               May 10, 1864

Sir:

For you information and government in the inspection and receipt of Warner Carbines, I enclose a copy of a letter to Mr. Warner granting him an extension of forty days. You will please return to Mr. Warner the 500 Carbines already received that he may make the alterations suggested in Maj. Dyer's report, a copy of which was sent you April 22nd.

Geo D. Ramsay
Brig. Gen. Ch. of Ord.

James Warner   Ordnance Office
Springfield, Mass.   May 10, 1864

Sir

Your letter of April 27th requesting an extension of time for delivering the carbines due under your contract of January 13th, 1864, was received, referred to the Secretary of War, and is now returned to this office with instructions to grant you an extension of forty days from May 1st. Col. Thornton has been notified that you are to alter the 500 carbines already delivered by you.

Geo D. Ramsay
Brig. Gen. Ch. of Ord.

The first clear indication of Warner's contract objectives and production intentions were outlined in his letter to the Ordnance Office on May 19th, 1864:[32]

Springfield, Mass.
May 19, 1864

Capt. Geo T. Balch
Ordnance Department
Washington, DC

My Dear Sir:

I have in process of manufacture at Springfield twenty five hundred of the Warner Carbine, in addition to the five hundred already delivered, a considerable portion of which have been partially inspected and are nearly completed. The Greene Rifle Works at Worcester, under a contract with me have in process of manufacture three thousand of the Warner Carbine (with some improvements) part of which have been inspected under a previous arrangement with the Ordnance Department.

I now desire that an inspector shall be continued at both places until the inspection of all the above named carbines is completed.

Please give the necessary instructions therefore.

James Warner

General Ramsay responded the following day:[33]

James Warner Esq.   Ordnance Office
Springfield, Mass.   Washington - May 20, 1864

Sir

I have to acknowledge and receipt of your letter of 19th inst. and in reply would state that Col. Thornton, Inspector of Small Arms, has been directed to continue the inspection at your works in Springfield and at the Greene Rifle Works with the distinct understanding expressed in the letter to you from this office dated March 1st, 1864 that this inspection does not render it in the least obligatory upon the part of Government to receive these arms.

With this full understanding the inspections will be continued until the 3000 carbines at the Greene Rifle Works and the 2500 at Springfield are finished.

Geo D. Ramsay
Br. Gen'l. Chf. Ord.

Ordnance Office
War Department
Washington, DC - May 20, 1864

Col. W. A. Thornton
Inspector of Contract Arms
240 Broadway, New York

Sir

A letter has been received from Mr. James Warner, Springfield Mass requesting that the inspector at his works in Springfield as well as the one at the Greene Rifle Works may be continued.

In reference thereto I would state that by a letter from this office dated March 1st, 1864 you were directed to detail a sub-inspector to inspect but not to receive the work on the Warner Carbine to the number of say 3,000 then in progress of manufacture at the Greene Rifle Works.

You will be pleased to continue the inspector at these works until the completion of the inspection of 3,000 with the distinct understanding expressed in the letter of March 1st that the Government is not involved in any obligation whatever to receive these arms after they are inspected.

With this <u>same</u> <u>understanding</u> you will be pleased to continue the inspector at the works in Springfield — who will inspect 2,000 carbines now being made — which are <u>additional</u> to the 1,000 to be furnished under contract of January 13th, 1864.

George D. Ramsay
Brig. Gen'l. & Chief Ord.

Panic must have overcome Warner on June 11th when the inspector at Springfield was recalled by Colonel Thornton. One can only imagine his concern that with his contract now expired, five hundred carbines already had been delivered to the government and the remaining five hundred unable to be accepted. He quickly wrote General Ramsay:[34]

Springfield, June 11, 1864

Brig. Gen'l. Geo D. Ramsay
Chief Ordnance
War Department
Washington

Dear Sir:

I have this morning received instructions from the Government Inspector at my works that he received notice today of his removal under the directions of Col. Thornton, not withstanding your intimation contained in your letter under date May 20th, 1864 of your instructions for the inspectors continuance. The extension of my contract for forty days for the completion of the one thousand carbines expired yesterday. The guns were in the inspectors hands yesterday and are packing in their boxes today and will be immediately forwarded to the New York Arsenal. The withdrawal of the inspector will stop this operation, and being in opposition to your directions, must arise from error which I cannot think, from the universal regularity in correspondence with the War Department originated in Washington. Your rectifying the mistake will oblige.

James Warner

Finally on June 19th, with his last five hundred carbines crated and ready for shipment, Warner again bypassed Colonel Thornton and wrote directly to General Ramsay requesting delivery instructions. His answer arrived three days later:[35]

Jas Warner Esq.   Ordnance Office
Springfield, Mass.   Washington, DC
                                June 20, 1864
Sir:

I have to acknowledge the receipt of your letter of 17th inst. and in reply say that you will be pleased to send the 500 carbines therein to the New York Arsenal Capt. S. Crispin commanding.

Geo. D. Ramsay
Br. Gen'l. Chf. Ord

Warner had just forwarded his arms to Captain Crispin when Ramsay offered him a second contract for cartridges that was twice the size of the first:[36]

Jas Warner Esq.   Ordnance Office
Springfield, Mass.   Washington - June 27, 1864
Sir:

Referring to your letter of May 7th in which you stated you were "erecting machinery" and works for the manufacture of cartridges suitable for your carbine". I have to request that you state at what price you will make and at what rate you will deliver 1,000,000 Warner Carbine Cartridges.

Geo D. Ramsay
Br. Genl. Chf. Ord.

Before Warner could respond to this latest offer problems began to reappear with the payment of the five hundred carbines recently sent to Capt. Crispin. Warner's concern over the situation was clearly evident in his telegram to Ramsay on June 29th:[37]

Office US Military Telegraph
War Department
Washington - June 29, 1864

General Ramsay
Chief of Ordnance

General:

My carbines last ordered are delivered to Capt. Crispin. Col. Thornton declines to certify without orders from you. Please send order by telegraph.

Jas Warner

Ramsay must have been disturbed about this situation for he sent Colonel Thornton a telegraph later that same day directing him to provide a report on the facts of the case.[38]

Back at Springfield

Warner obviously was far from ready to produce cartridges when he wrote his response to Ramsay's request. Rather than provide an answer, one he probably did not have, he chose to give an update on the progress of the cartridge production facilities he was erecting:[39]

Springfield - June 30, 1864

Brig. Gen. Geo. D. Ramsay
Chief Ordnance
War Department
Washington

Dear Sir

I have to acknowledge the receipt of your letter under date the 27th inst., requesting to know the price, and at what rate I could undertake to deliver (1,000,000) one million Warner's Carbine Cartridges.

The last machine of those made at my works necessary for the purpose of their manufacture will be in a few days completed, and a Mr. Colton of this city will then have works in efficient condition for the execution of extensive orders for these cartridges. The Mr. Colton above mentioned, has made arrangement with me, to manufacture in any quantity the cartridges for my carbine and with the very complete machinery and establishment he will start with I have not the least doubt of his fulfilling his engagements. I have taken the liberty to give him a letter of introduction to you, as it is his intention to visit Washington in the subject of your letter to me of the 27th inst.

Jas Warner
by Geo L. Robinson

Warner's evasiveness quickly became academic for on the same day C.D. Leet, one of the largest metallic cartridge manufacturers of the day, was sent a contract to produce and deliver one million Warner cartridges at a price of $26 per thousand.

The Ordnance Office had apparently realized the impact a shortage of cartridges would have on the operational effectiveness of the Warner Carbine and had approached C.D. Leet as early as April 22nd, 1864, with a proposal to manufacture Warner cartridges. Warner's obvious inability to produce both carbines and cartridges with any regularity apparently prompted the government to accept the C.D. Leet proposal. As a result, Warner was never again requested to provide cartridges for his carbine.

On July 2nd Colonel Thornton forwarded his explanation of why he had refused to certify Warner's last delivery of the five hundred carbines:[40]

Office of Inspector of Contract Arms
240 Broadway
New York - July 2nd, 1864

General G. B. Ramsay
Chief of Ordnance

Sir:

In answer to your endorsement of the 30th and Warner's Telegram of the 29th of June just received, I have the honor to report that Mr. Warners contracts for carbines dated January the 13th expired on the 1st of May 1864, and by your instructions of the 10th of May, the time was extended to June the 10th, 1864.

As he failed to have his arms ready for delivery on the 10th of June, his contract came under the provisions of your instructions of the 20 of May 1864 which directs "the continuation of the inspections of carbines at the Armory of Mr. Warner at Springfield Mass. until 2000 should be examined, with the distinct understanding that the government is not involved in any obligation whatever to receive the carbines after "inspection".

On the 16th of June, Mr. Warner called on me at Springfield where I was on duty, to know if I could accept his carbines. I informed him that his contract expired on the 10th of June, and as he had failed to deliver in the time allowed, I had no authority to go beyond the time granted for the delivery of the carbines.

On the 23rd of June Mr. Warner informed me by letter that he had forwarded 500 carbines to my address and on the 27th he called on me to accept the arms which I declined to do without your authority. He then stated that he had been ordered by you to ship them to Captain Crispin, and presented the usual certificates for payments which were signed by the Sub-Inspector then on duty at his armory which he desired me to approve. I requested him to let me see your order for the shipment of the carbines to Captain Crispin which would enable me to approve the inspections. He informed me that he had not the order with him, and I advised him to telegraph at once to his Armory to have the order sent here without delay, so that I might act on it, in approving the certificate.

It came the next day when I was absent on duty and I have neither seen or heard further from Mr. Warner on the subject. If he had shown me your order to forward the carbines to Captain Crispin I would have approved the inspection and I so advised him at the time he visited my office.

W. A. Thornton
Col. of Ordnance Inspections

Since writing the above the certificates have been presented and I have approved them.

W.A. Thornton
Col. of Ordnance

Additional Carbines

Resolution of this problem appeared to satisfy all parties for Warner received payment for the last 500 carbines on July 28, 1864. No further correspondence occurred until late October. And it would seem that up until that time Warner had been hard at work assembling additional arms. Despite the fact that he had fulfilled his original contract four months prior, his letter dated October 22nd to the new Chief of Ordnance, General Alexander B. Dyer, reads as if he still had a contract obligation to supply carbines:[41]

Brig. General A.B. Dyer   Springfield Arms Company
Chief of Ordnance   Springfield - Oct. 22, 1864
Washington, DC

Dear Sir

I shall in a few days have five hundred carbines packed for shipment they being now under inspection. I shall feel obliged by your forwarding instructions to Col. Thornton, Chief Inspector Contract Arms, to receive the shipment as on the last occasion there was some difficulty and delay, from the absence of instructions from Washington. Would you inform me if the under mentioned address of the boxes is correct at the present time or whether there has been any recent change from the last address.

Jas Warner
by Geo L. Robinson

Capt S. Crispin
Comm'g, New York Arsenal
Care of Major S. Van Vliet
Q-MAST USA
New York

Dyer must have thought Warner had a contract for those guns and forwarded his letter to Thornton with the following endorsement:[42]

Respectfully referred to Col. W.A. Thornton who will please make arrangement for the shipment of the carbines.

A.B. Dyer
Brig. Gen. Chief of Ord.
Nov. 11, 1864

(National Archives)

Brigadier General Alexander B. Dyer.

Upon receipt, Thornton made the following notation below Dyers endorsement:[43]

Pursuant to the endorsement hereon I have this day requested Mr. Warner to forward the 500 Carbines through the Q-Masters Departments to Captain A.R. Buffington, Commander New York Arsenal, Office of Inspector of Contract Arms, New York City.

November 12, 1864
W. A. Thornton
Col. of Ordnance

Warners bluff, if that is what it was, had worked. He proceeded to deliver an additional five hundred carbines. Apparently he was anxious to have Thornton accept delivery of the five hundred carbines and wrote Dyer again on October 29th.[44]

Springfield
October 29th, 1864

Brig. Gen. A.B. Dyer
Chief Ordnance
Washington DC

Dear sir

I wrote to you under date the 22 inst. in reference to the five hundred carbines now inspecting and requesting your instructions to Col. Thornton to receive the same. Not having received a reply I have to request your attention to my communication of that date.

Jas Warner
by Geo L. Robinson

What prompted Dyer to write Warner in early November 1864 requesting the manufacture of an iron frame carbine is unknown. However his requirements of using an iron breech and chambering the arm to the Spencer cartridge are quite specific. It is interesting to note that this iron frame model was a request by the government made subsequent to the full scale production of both the Warner and Greene model carbines and not, as some would believe, an evolutionary or production improvement of either model.[45]

Mr. Jas Warner   Ordnance Office
Springfield, Mass.   War Department
                 Washington - Nov. 4th, 1864
Sir

I have to request that you will at your earliest convenience inform this office how soon you could be prepared to furnish this Department with carbines of your pattern having an iron breech piece instead of brass and of a caliber suitable for the Spencer Carbine Cartridge.

A.B. Dyer, Br. Gen'l
Chief of Ordnance

On November 5th General Dyer made an inquiry as to the price Warner would charge for an additional two thousand carbines. Warner's reply was mailed out promptly on November 6th, 1864:[46]

Brig. Gen. A.B. Dyer Springfield - Nov. 8th, 1864
Chief of Ordnance
War Department

Dear Sir

In reply to your communication received this day in reference to the price that I will furnish two thousand Warner Carbines — I beg to note that I will supply the Government with that number at twenty dollars each with appendages.

Jas Warner
by Geo L. Robinson

Future Orders

Warner probably assumed he had a new contract and that any subsequent payment for carbines would conform with the new twenty dollar offer. One week later, on November 15th, Warner completed delivery of the five hundred additional carbines from his Springfield facility and forwarded certificates to Colonel Thornton in New York City.[47] Two days later he forwarded to General Dyer the price at which he would furnish his "iron breech" carbines suitable for the Spencer cartridge.[48]

The prospect of future carbine orders could have prompted Warner to have J.W. Emery, President of the Greene Rifle Works make an offer on November 16th to furnish "three thousand carbines at a rate of twenty to fifty a day and at a price the same as paid James Warner."[49]

The following day Warner himself offered to supply ten to fifteen thousand arms at a cost of twenty-two dollars each with the first delivery three months from the date of any contract.[50] With hopes of future orders all but complete, Warner wrote General Dyer on November 22nd, 1864:[51]

Springfield - Nov. 22nd, 1864
General A.B. Dyer
Chief of Ordnance
Washington

Dear Sir

The United States Government is requested to receive from the Greene Rifle Works three thousand carbines, the same as if the carbines were manufactured by me, and pay James W. Emery, President of the Greene Rifle Works for the same at the price of twenty dollars per carbine, the same as though the carbines were received from me.

James Warner

On November 28th Warner received payment for his five hundred carbine delivery of November 15th. However, as early as October 29th there had been indications that something was delaying payment for this delivery. On that date Warner wrote Dyer stating that he had not yet received a reply to his request to have Colonel Thornton receive the five hundred carbines. On November 26th Thornton must have been aware that this most recent carbine delivery was improper because no contract had been executed and asked Dyer for instructions. On November 28th Warner received his payment certificates signed by Colonel Thornton marked down from twenty to eighteen dollars! This was enough to cause Warner to write Dyer again:[52]

Brig. Gen. A.B. Dyer   Springfield - Nov. 28th, 1864
Chief of Ordnance
War Department
Washington D.C.

Dear Sir

I have to enclose your copy of my letter addressed to you on the 8th inst. in reply to your favor of the 5th requesting to know of what price I could furnish two thousand of my carbines to the Department. Under date the 12th inst. I received a letter from Col. W.A. Thornton stating he has instructions from you to receive the carbines I had ready (viz 500) I forwarded the same in accordance from this place on the 15th and I am surprised this day to have my certificates for the carbines signed by Col. Thornton returned to me, but with the price of $20 ea., altered to that of $18. This must doubtless arise from Col. Thornton not having received the necessary intimation of the price of the two thousand carbines. I shall feel obliged by your early attention in rectifying this matter.

Jas Warner
by Geo L. Robinson

General Dyer received Warner's letter on the 30th and made an immediate inquiry into what had happened. Colonel Thornton's reply was that he was simply following the instructions given to him on March 1st, 1864. How the referenced date got changed to March 21st is unclear, but that mistake only further confused the issue:[53]

Col. W.A. Thornton   Ordnance Office
Inspector of Contract Arms   War Department
240 Broadway, NY   Washington, DC
                           Nov. 30, 1864
Sir

Not being able to find on record the letter of March 21 — the date which you state you were authorized "to inspect but not receive Warners Carbine" nor of any application from Mr. Warner to that effect,

I have to request that you will send as soon as possible, a copy of said instruction, and any other information you may possess on the subject.

> A.B. Dyer
> Brig. Gen. Chief of Ord.

Thornton's reply was prompt.[54]

> Office of Inspector of Contract Arms
> 240 Broadway
> New York - Dec. 1st, 1864
>
> General A.B. Dyer
> Chief of Ordnance
> Sir
>
> I have the honor to acknowledge the receipt of your instructions of the 30th inst. and I herewith enclose copies of orders directing me to inspect, but not accept carbines then being manufactured by James Warner at Springfield and Worcester, Mass.
>
> > W.A. Thornton
> > Colonel of Ordnance Inspections

It was now clear to General Dyer that a mistake had been made in the decision to direct acceptance of the five hundred guns. He wrote Warner and attempted to explain the situation. The same day he gave Thornton specific instruction not to accept any more of Warner's carbines.[55]

> Mr. James Warner   War Department
> Springfield, Mass.   Washington - Dec. 3, 1864
> Sir
>
> I have to acknowledge your letter of 28th inst. in which you state that Col. Thornton had given you certificates for 500 of your carbines fixing the price of $18.00 instead of $20.00 and asking correction of the error.
>
> In reply I have to state that I find no record of any order given to you for the 2,000 carbines you referred to and in the absence of that order Col. Thornton has no authority to receive them at any higher price that what he has done; that being the price named in your contract of January last. If you have received such an order it was sent off without being recorded, and in that case I have to request that you send the original to this office.
>
> On the 22nd of October last, you wrote to this office stating that in a few days you would have 500 carbines packed for shipment. Without investigating the circumstances your letter was referred to Col. Thornton with an endorsement for him to make arrangements for shipping the 500 carbines under the supposition that they were part of your original contract.
>
> On the 5th of November you were asked to state the price at which you would furnish 2,000 carbines. You replied on the 8th naming $20 as the price. This

letter by accident was mislaid and did not come to light until search was made for it in receiving a copy of it with yours of 28th November.

> On the proposition no action has been taken and the subject is under consideration.
>
> > A.B. Dyer Brig. Gen'l.
> > Chief of Ordnance

> Col. W. A. Thornton   Ordnance Office
> Inspector of Contract Arms   War Department
> No. 240 Broadway, New York   Washington DC
>   Dec. 3, 1864
> Sir
>
> In reply to your letter of 26th inst. I have to state that the Warner carbines which you report as being under inspection at Springfield and Worcester, are not to be accepted by you without special instructions to that effect.
>
> > A.B. Dyer
> > Brig. Gen. Chief of Ord.

Warner promptly returned the altered certificates in a letter to Dyer on December 5th:[56]

> Springfield - Dec. 5th, 1864
>
> Brig. Gen. A.B. Dyer
> Chief of Ordnance
> War Department
> Washington DC
> Dear Sir
>
> I beg to refer you to my letter of the 28th ultimo at present unreplied to and to expedite my receiving the certificates of the five hundred carbines forwarded as instructed on the 15th inst. to the New York Arsenal. I herewith enclose you the certificates altered in price from $20 to $18 each by Col. Thornton, and to which my letter of the 28th inst. has reference. I shall feel obliged by your instructions to Col. Thornton to have these certificates rectified as the delay has caused me inconvenience.
>
> > James Warner

Dyer received the letter two days later. To insure that Thornton did not counter his plan, Dyer explained the proposition he was about to offer Warner:[57]

> Col. W. A. Thornton   Ordnance Office
> Inspector of Arms   War Department
> 240 Broadway, NY   Washing DC - Dec. 7, 1864
> Sir
>
> In reply to your letter of 26th inst. I have to state that you will not continue to accept the Warner Carbines beyond the 500 authorized 14th inst. without special instructions to that effect.
>
> A proposition has been made to Mr. Warner for the purpose of 2500 @ $20 provided he will ream them to receive the Spencer cartridges. If he accepts the offer you will be duly advised.

The order of 14th inst. for the shipment of 500 carbines which you have received having been given after receipt of a proposition from Mr. Warner to furnish them @ $20 each; he is entitled to that price for these 500 and the certificate which you gave him for them has been altered accordingly.

A.B. Dyer
Brig. Gen. Chf. of Ord.

Mr. James Warer   Ordnance Office
Springfield Mass.   War Department
                          Washington - Dec. 7, 1864
Sir

Your letter of 5th inst. with the altered certificate of inspection is received. There is nothing on file in this office showing why you should be paid $20.00 instead of $18.00 for the 500 carbines and since Col. Thornton was not furnished with instructions as to the price you were to be allowed, he could therefore not give certificates for a higher amount than those previously delivered. But as it now appears upon investigating the subject that Col. Thornton was not instructed to receive those 500 carbines until after the reception of your letter of 8th November in which you offered to furnish 2,000 at $20.00 each, the Department will pay you for these 500 at that price and your account has been corrected accordingly, and will be sent to the Treasury for payment. You will understand however that the payment for these 500 carbines is not to be understood as an acceptance of the offer to furnish 2,000 at that price and Col. Thornton has been instructed accordingly. But if you will ream the chambers of 2,500 of your carbines to receive the cartridge now used in the Spencer Carbine giving one hundredth of an inch taper to it, the Department will give you an order for that number at twenty dollars ($20.00) each.

A.B. Dyer Brig. Gen.
Chief of Ordnance

On the same day that Dyer offered Warner a new contract, C.W. Emery, President of the Greene Rifle Works offered to provide Dyer with three thousand of Warner's pattern carbines:[58]

The Greene Rifle Works
Junction Shop
Worcester, Mass. - Dec. 7, 1864
Gen. A.B. Dyer
Chief of Ordnance
Washington

My Dear Sir,
On Nov. 16th I wrote you from New York that the Greene Rifle Works would, the following week, have completed ready for shipment five hundred carbines of the Warner pattern, that the balance of the three thousand commenced would be finished at the rate of from twenty to fifty a day, and desired to know

Worcester, Mass., Dec. 7 1864

*Gen. A. B. Dyer
Chief of ordnance
Washington*

The official stationery of the Greene Rifle Works, shown here in a letter dated December 7, 1864.   (National Archives)

if the Government wanted the same. We have had no reply to that letter. We have now completed and boxed up ready for shipment the five hundred guns above named, and desire to know, as soon as may be, whether or not the Government is going to take them. If the Government does not take them we can sell them for a larger price than we have offered them to you. An early reply is respectfully requested. My address is Boston, 39 State Street.

James W. Emery, President
Greene Rifle Works

A Second Contract

On December 10th Warner accepted Dyer's new offer to deliver 2,500 carbines, "reamed up" to accept the Spencer 56-56 cartridge currently in use. On December 14th Dyer responded to Emery's letter offering to provide three thousand carbines of the Warner pattern. Whether or not Emery really had another buyer for the carbine is unknown. In any case, Emery forwarded Dyers response to Warner, indicating that only Warner had authority to contract with the Government. On December 19th Warner wrote Dyer requesting he increase the most recent order to cover the additional three thousand guns being made at Worcester:[59]

Springfield, Mass.
December 19, 1864

Gen'l. A.B. Dyer
Chief of Ordnance
Washington DC

My Dear Sir
I am today in receipt of a copy of your letter to J.W. Emery, President Greene Rifle Works at Worcester under date December 14th. I have nearly completed and ready fifteen hundred carbines in my own works and the Greene Rifle Works have three thou-

sand (one thousand of which will be ready to ship this week). The balance will be completed during the next sixty or seventy days. My purpose is to ask if you will increase the order which you have sent so as to cover the whole of the three thousand being finished at the Greene Rifle Works.

James Warner

P.S. I have an improvement on my iron breech, the model of which will be done this week which I think will please you and which I hope to show you here.

Yours
J.W.

It is interesting to note the post script indicating that development of the iron frame carbine was progressing and proceeding parallel with the production of the brass frame models.

Despite the fact that he had already accepted the government contract for twenty five hundred guns. Warner refused to give up and persisted in requesting that Dyer increase the carbine order so as to cover the entire three thousand arms being finished at the Greene Rifle Works. Dyer however was having no part of it, and forwarded Warners second contract unchanged to Edwin M. Stanton the Secretary of War on December 31st, 1864.[60] Warner received his second contract on January 4, 1865 and promptly requested delivery instructions for the carbines he had already completed.[61]

Springfield - Jan. 7th, 1865

Brig. Gen. A.B. Dyer
Chief Ordnance
War Department
Washington, DC

Dear Sir

I have to acknowledge the receipt of yours under date the 4th inst. transmitting Duplicate Copy of a contract for 2,500 carbines. I have 500 of these carbines inspected and packed for shipment and shall have in a week or ten days 500 more. I shall feel obliged by your instructions to Col. W. A. Thornton in reference to the receipt of these carbines ready for delivery, under the contract not having heard from him on the subject.

Jas Warner
by Geo L. Robinson

General Dyer promptly responded to Warners letter and furnished Colonel Thornton instructions.[62]

Mr. James Warner   Ordnance Office
Springfield, Mass.   War Department
                    Washington - Jan. 10, 1865
  Sir
    I have to acknowledge the receipt of yours of the 7th inst. in relation to carbines ready for inspection and in relation to carbines ready for inspection and in reply I have to state that the 500 carbines reported by you ready for shipment together with these now in process of completion will have to be inspected in order to ascertain if they conform to the stipulations of your contract of 2,500 carbines dated December 26, 1864, as regards the capacity of the chambers to receive the Spencer Carbine Cartridge. Col. Thornton has this day been notified to proceed with their inspection.

A.B. Dyer Brig. Gen'l.
Chief of Ordnance

Col. W. A. Thornton   Ordnance Office
Inspector of Contract Arms   War Department
New York   Washington, DC
                              Jan. 10, 1865
Sir
    Mr. James Warner, Springfield, Mass. reports that he has ready for inspection 500 Warner's Carbines and in process of completion 500 additional. As these are to be received under the contract of December 26th, 1864 for 2500 your attention is called to the stipulation of the contract, providing that the chamber shall be made of such size as to receive the cartridge now used in the Spencer Carbine.

    You will proceed with their inspection as early as you can conveniently do so.

A.B. Dyer
Brig. Gen.
Chief of Ordnance

Final Deliveries

By mid-February Warner's deliveries of carbines from both the Springfield and Worcester facilities began to be consistent. In accordance with the stipulation in his second contract to have carbines "delivered at the armory where fabricated as rapidly as possible" Warner made deliveries at his Springfield facility of five hundred and eight hundred arms on the 2nd and 27th of February respectively. Concurrently the Greene Rifle Works made deliveries at Worcester of five hundred carbines on February 18th and another seven hundred on March 15, 1865.[63] The March delivery completed the second contract for Warners breech loading carbine.

The Civil War was almost over. Accordingly, government contracts were either not being issued or were in the process of being rescinded. James Warner's brass frame carbine was no exception.

In early March 1865 Warner approached the Ordnance Office with a request to be reimbursed for the cost of drilling vent holes in the breech frame of his carbines — a modification that had been directed by the government. General Dyer ordered Colonel Thornton to honor Warner's request of March 3rd even though the original understanding was that this modification "would materially improve the arm without adding to the price".[64]

Col. W. A. Thornton
240 Broadway New York

Ordnance Office
War Department
Washington DC
Mar. 3, 1965

Sir

In answer to your letter of the 2nd inst. I have to state that Mr. Warner is entitled to the payment of a fair charge for drilling vent holes in the breech frame of his carbines and other charges incurred in making this modification, and you are requested to approve his account accordingly.

A.B. Dyer
Brig. Gen. Chf. of Ord.

The final record of Warner's carbine and its service with the United States Government is contained in an offer on October 30th, 1865 by the Greene Rifle Works of 39 State Street, Boston, Massachusetts, requesting to sell eighteen hundred carbines at twenty dollars each.[65] These arms must have been the remainder of the three thousand that were produced, but only twelve hundred of which were purchased, when the second contract was completed. By now however the war was over and the Army of the Potomac was awash in surplus weapons. Accordingly, the offer was refused.

Leather carbine cartridge box with wooden block drilled to hold 56-56 Spencer cartridges. A Warner cartridge box would only have differed in the size of the holes drilled in the wooden block. (Author's Collection)

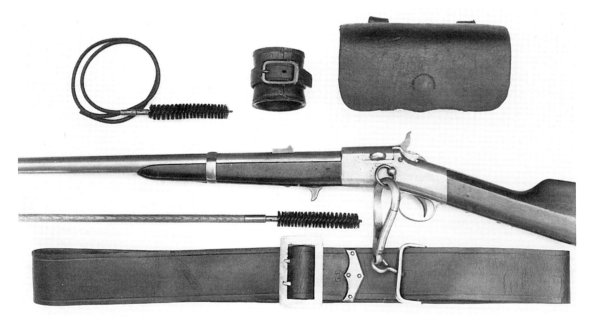

Carbine accouterments: (Top to bottom) bristle brush with leather thong for field cleaning; leather carbine boot; carbine cartridge box; Warner carbine, Serial No. 857, rechambered for the 56-56 Spencer cartridge; "garrison" cleaning rod and bristle brush; black bridle leather carbine sling with swivel and snap hook. (Author's Collection)

CHAPTER 4

AMMUNITION

The Warner rimfire was a proprietary cartridge developed by the inventor. It was loaded with 35 grains of black powder and held a .515 inch diameter, 360 grain lead bullet.

As early as 1863, James Warner must have had a reasonable supply of ammunition for testing his carbines, however there is no evidence that Warner ever had any capability to fabricate his own ammunition. It would therefore seem probable that he contracted with one of the cartridge makers in his area to fill his needs. Whether that supplier was Crittenden and Tibbals, D.C. Sage, or C.D. Leet is unknown. However, speculation that Leet, also of Springfield, Massachusetts, and a major supplier at the time of specialty rimfire ammunition was James Warner's supplier, is not entirely out of the question.

The Warner cartridge.

Bullet size:	*.515*
Bullet weight:	*360 grain*
Powder charge:	*35 grain*
Rim diameter:	*.606*
Head diameter:	*.529*
Mouth diameter:	*.530*
Cartridge length:	*.860*
Overall length:	*1.52*

Supply Problems

James Warner's inability to produce carbines rapidly and in quantity was only exceeded by his inability to supply ammunition for those same arms. As early as March 1864, it was apparent that inspectors at the Worcester facility could not complete their proofing for lack of a suitable supply of ammunition.[1]

In mid-April 1864, Warner offered "to produce" half a million cartridges at a cost of $25 per thousand. On April 27th, he made a second offer to sell ten thousand cartridges he currently had on hand for $26 per thousand.[2] The government quickly accepted his offer at a cost of $25 per thousand, forwarded a contract and directed that he ship the cartridges he had available to the New York Arsenal.

However, on May 7th 1864 Warner declined the 500,000 cartridge contract he had just received. He stated he had shipped 9,000 cartridges in 9 boxes, but needed to reserve 1,000 for his own use in proofing his carbines. His reason for declining the government contract was that the cartridge makers in his area were so extended with orders that they could not accept his.[3]

Still without a supplier of cartridges for Warner's Carbine, and with the hope that Warner himself would soon erect his own cartridge works, General Ramsay approached him on June 27th with an order to produce one million cartridges! However, Warner's sidestepping of the offer in his June 30th letter to Ramsay spelled an end of further proposals by the Ordnance Department for Warner to supply cartridges for his carbines.

C.D. Leet

Despite the fact that a factory explosion and fire on March 16, 1864, had temporarily caused C.D. Leet to suspend production, the Ordnance Department nevertheless approached him in mid April 1864 about the possibility of producing ammunition for the Warner carbine. His response was positive:[4]

Springfield, Mass   April 22, 1864
Brig. Gen. George D. Ramsay
Chief of Ordnance
Washington, D.C.

Sir

Your telegram with regard to cartridges for Warner's Carbine was duly received, but unavoidable absence from the city at the time and until now has precluded the possibility of an early reply.

I could be ready to commence the delivery of cartridges for Warner's Carbine in about six weeks. Should you be pleased to give me an order for them, the price which will be twenty-six dollars per mille. This price is based upon the present price of stock and material upon which there has within ten days been a considerable advance.

C.D. Leet

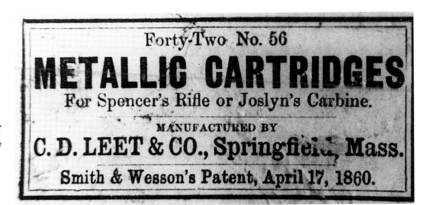

Cartridge box label for No. 56 metallic cartridges (56-56 Spencer) made by C.D. Leet, c. 1864.

P.S. I will put up the #56 [Spencer 56-56] cartridges designed under order of January 27 for Joslyn's Carbine, for Ballard's or Spencer's Carbine if you desire the change at twenty seven dollars per M. I shall get my works running again next week in full force and shall hope to give then 150 M per week. Shall I continue the delivery of the Joslyn cartridges?

CDL

With Warner's decline of offers to supply first 500,000 and later one million cartridges, the government decided to accept Leet's offer and forwarded him a contract to supply one million Warner cartridges. In a letter dated July 7, 1864 Leet states:[5]

The quintriplicate copy for one million of the Warner cartridges is this day received. I have accepted an order from Captain Crispin for 90,000 Cartridges for Warner's carbine to be delivered on or before the 1st day of August 1864 and I desire that this one shall take the place of the 100,000 which this contract with the Department calls for. If this is your understanding of the matter I am ready to go forward and execute the contract at once. Otherwise I must delay the first delivery until one or two weeks after the first of August.

C.D. Leet

By August 10th, however, Leet was having problems with his factory's delivery schedule and requested an extension of his first delivery until August 20th. The following week he stated that he had 100,000 Warner cartridges nearly ready for shipment.[6] He finally managed to make delivery of them by early September 1864.

By September 16th he again wrote General Ramsay explaining that a combination of the New England Fair and relocation to his new shop had delayed getting his new machines in operation and that a few more weeks would be necessary until he could again establish his production of cartridges.[7] These delays continued until late November when he finally began deliveries of Warner cartridges at a reliable rate.

A Decision to Standardize

By this time it was apparent that the Ordnance office's inquiry into Warner's ability to manufacture "an Iron breech carbine of the caliber suitable for the Spencer carbine cartridge" clearly illustrated their desire to standardize ammunition types. This idea was not entirely new. As early as September 16th, 1863 a board of Ordnance Officers, chaired by Lieutenant Colonel Hagner had been formed under the authority of Special Order 410. One of their charters was "to establish a uniform caliber and length of barrel for all carbines to be hereafter used in the service". Their recommendations were that for all future orders for carbines of a kind <u>not</u> now used, the diameter of the bore be .52 inches, barrel length be 22 inches, total weight of the arm not exceed eight nor be less than six pounds and the weight of the powder charge be one tenth of that of the ball. It should be noted that Warner's carbine and the ammunition it used met all of these specifications.

The board further recommended that "the following named carbines be made with bores .52 inch diameter; Sharps, Gibbs, Starr, Spencer, Joslyn, Sharps & Hankins and Ballard. The first three of these would then be able to use the Sharps cartridge, while the last four would be able to use the Spencer cartridge.

Mention was also made of various other carbines presently in service using particular cartridges, but concluded that modification of those carbines would only cause confusion due to the multiplicity of cartridges for the same arm. Modification was, therefore, not recommended.[8]

Why the Ordnance Department overlooked this very specific and logical recommendation and proceeded to issue James Warner his first contract for carbines chambered for the Warner, versus Spencer cartridge, is unclear. However, by November 1864, the Federal Ordnance Department was already evaluating the feasibility of rechambering the Warner carbine to fire Spencer ammunition.

What amounted to the final nail in the coffin for the Warner cartridge was a letter from Captain Crispin at the New York Arsenal.[9]

> US Ordnance Agency
> 45 Worth Street
> New York - Dec. 16th, 1864
>
> Brig. Genl. A.B. Dyer
> Chief of Ordnance
> Washington, D.C.
>
> General;
>
> I have the honor to acknowledge the receipt of your instruction of the 14th inst. to order 500,000 cartridges for Warner's carbine and in reply would state that I have now in my file unexecuted, your instructions of the 7th ultimo to purchase 1,000,000 of the same ammunition. The only party who has facilities for the fabrication of these cartridges is Mr. C.D. Leet, who has an existing contract with the bureau for 1,000,000 of which 800,000 are still due. His present production is 50,000 per week and under instructions from this office he is making every effort to increase this quantity at the earliest possible date. At present however the production of "Warners" cartridges can only be increased by diminishing the production of "Spencers", a measure which in view of the large unexecuted order in my file for the latter (about one million) I have not felt justified in adopting.
>
> Be pleased to instruct me if the demand for the "Warner" ammunition is sufficiently urgent to warrant such a course.
>
> I would state in this connection that 100,000 Warner cartridges have been sent to the Nashville Depot since the 22nd ultimo and that the present production of the Spencer cartridge is about 600,000 per week from all sources.
>
> Crispin
> Capt. of Ordnance

The decision was now relatively simple. Experiments at the Washington D.C. Arsenal were proving that the Warner carbine could be successfully rechambered to fire the Spencer 56-56 rimfire cartridge. Deliveries of Warner cartridges were delayed and to accelerate them would adversely affect deliveries of the Spencer cartridges — the ammunition that was fast becoming the standard for breechloading arms.

Accordingly, no further orders for Warner cartridges would be issued and the decision would be made to have government armorers at the Washington Arsenal rechamber those Warner carbines on hand (approximately 550) to take the Spencer cartridge.

It is important to mention that as early as November 1864, G.W. Dudley, master armorer at the Washington Arsenal was experimenting with rechambering the Warner to fire Spencer ammunition, and that General Dyer requested a quote from Warner on his ability to make an iron breech carbine suitable for the "Spencer carbine cartridge". Additionally, in December Dyer offered Warner a second contract for carbines provided he ream the chambers of the guns to the cartridge now used in the Spencer carbine.

All of these references were to the 56-56 (#56) Spencer cartridge and not the 56-50 Spencer cartridge. This is further substantiated by the fact that the first delivery of 56-50 Spencer ammunition to the government did not occur until mid-February 1865![10]

Cartridge comparison.
(L to R) .50 Warner, .56 Spencer and .50 Spencer by Sage Ammunition Works. (Lou Behling Collection)

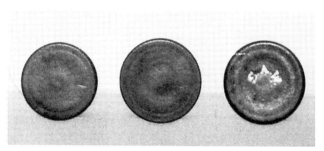

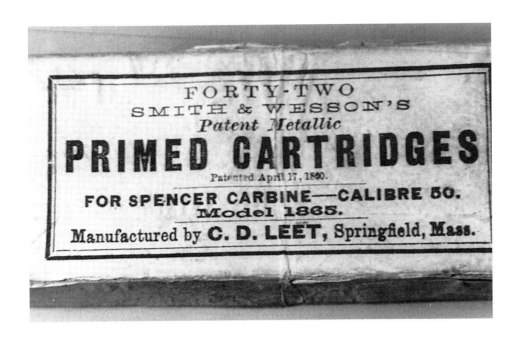

Cartridge box labels for C.D. Leet (above) and Sage
Ammunition Works (below) metallic cartridges c. 1865.

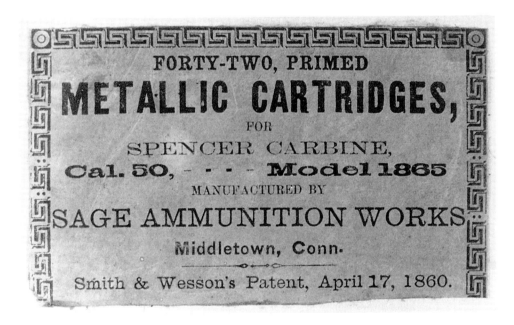

CHAPTER 5

TEST AND EVALUATION

Army Ordnance Test and Evaluation

By 1864, the number of different types of breechloading carbines in service prompted the Ordnance Department to order tests to evaluate them. Accordingly, on March 8th, 1864, Major Alexander B. Dyer, Commanding Officer at the Springfield Armory forwarded his first report on experiments with small arms.[1] His reports regarding Warner's carbine follow:[2]

> Seventh report on Breech loading Carbines made my Major A.B. Dyer assisted by Lt. Smoot at Springfield Armory 1864.
>
> Springfield Armory
> April 16, 1864
>
> Brig. Gen. George Ramsay
> Chief of Ordnance
> Washington, D.C.
>
> Sir
>
> In consequence of bad weather and want of cartridges only 125 rounds have been fired during the present week.
>
> In consequence of the explosion at Leet's Cartridge facility a few weeks ago Mr. Leet has not been able to supply the primed copper cases as rapidly as they are needed. Swaged balls of different diameter have been prepared for the 44" and 49" caliber and some Lancaster rifled barrels have been prepared.
>
> In firing Warner's breech loading carbine it was found when the copper case burst, that the escape of gas at the breech frequently threw open the breech piece with great violence and the two carbines were rendered unserviceable after a few rounds.
>
> Mr. Warner drilled a hole about a quarter of an inch in diameter in the receiver to allow the gas to escape, and it appears to have corrected the evil.
>
> I recommend that all the carbines shall be altered in that way before being issued to troops.
>
> A.B. Dyer
> Major, Ordnance

> Thirteenth report on Breech Loading Carbines made by Major A.B. Dyer assisted by Lt. Smoot at Springfield Armory 1864.[3]
>
> Springfield Armory
> May 28, 1864
>
> Brig. Gen'l G.A. Ramsay
> Chief of Ordnance
> Washington, D.C.
>
> Sir:
>
> During the past week 1,248 rounds have been fired including 264 from Stevens Breech Loading Carbine, and 100 rounds from rifle markets.
>
> The 24 and 34 inch twists have now been compared up to 1,000 rounds without cleaning. The rate of failing is about the same in both, while as regards accuracy there is a decided superiority in the short twist especially at the longer range.
>
> The Ballard, Sharps & Hankins and Warner carbines have also been subjected to a severe trial with heavy charges in order to ascertain the strength of their breech loading mechanism.
>
> The result is as follows: a Ballard and a Sharps & Hankins carbine were each fired with a charge of 50 grains of powder and 5 bullets weighing altogether 1,550 grains.
>
> The guard catch in both guns broke. The Ballard carbine being afterwards fired with 50 grains of powder and 8 bullets weighing altogether 2,680 grains sustained no further damage.
>
> A Warner carbine having a hole one quarter of an inch diameter drilled through the guard to provide for the escape of gas was fired with 50 grains of powder and 5 bullets weighing 1,550 grains. No damage was done to the gun although the cartridge shell burst at the shoulder. From this it would appear that a hole of that size is as large as should be drilled in the carbine to provide for the escape of gas from those shells that happen to burst.
>
> A considerable quantity of water was poured over the breech, lock, etc. of one of Joslyn's carbines which was loaded and it was well covered with mud thrown on with considerable force. The gun was left in that condition for 48 hours. It was found to be in good working order and was fired a number of times without difficulty.
>
> A.B. Dyer
> Major, Ordnance

During the summer of 1864, Major Dyer was promoted to Brigadier General and assumed the post as Chief of Ordnance in Washington.[4] Lieutenant Smoot continued the tests at Springfield:

> Twenty-ninth report on Breech Loading carbines.[5]
>
> Springfield Armory
> September 19, 1864

Brig. Gen'l. A.B. Dyer USA
Chief of Ordnance
Washington, D.C.

Sir

During the past week one hundred and eighty seven (187) rounds have been fired from Breech Loading Carbines including seventy five (75) rounds from the Warner Carbine.

Two guns were compared; one of which had thirty (30) grooves with a twist of one turn in thirty (30) inches and the other had a similar twist with three (3) grooves. The best shooting was done with the gun having thirty (30) grooves, but it is proposed to continue the comparison, as soon as the necessary cartridges can be obtained.

The Warner Carbine submitted for trial was a very much improved form of that weapon, but the barrel being defective only seventy five (75) rounds were fired.

A table of the firing is annexed.

W.S. Smoot
Lt. Ordnance

Date	Charge GRS		Number of		Distance to target	.44 Caliber 30 inch twist		Remarks
Sept.	Powder	Ball	Shots	Hits	Yards	3 GR	30 GR	
16th	45	280	24	23	500	15.4	11.8	Williams Center Primed Cartridge

Thirteenth report on Breech Loading Carbines.[6]

Springfield Armory
September 26, 1864

Brig. Gen'l. A.B. Dyer USA
Chief of Ordnance
Washington, D.C.

Sir

During the past week one hundred (100) rounds have been fired from Warners Breech Loading Carbine.

It has been impossible to continue the comparison between the two barrels having the one three (3) and the other thirty (30) grooves — owing to the want of cartridges.

A table of the firing is annexed.

W.S. Smoot
Lt. Ordnance

Date	Charge GRS		Number of		Distance to target	.50 Caliber 48 inch Twist	Remarks
Sept.	Powder	Ball	Shots	Hits	Yards		
23rd	35	360	25	17	500	18.9	Warners
23rd	35	360	25	17	500	29.1	Carbine
23rd	35	360	25	18	500	17.7	

Thirty-first report on Breech Loading Carbines.[7]

Springfield Armory
October 5, 1864

Brig. Gen'l. A.B. Dyer USA
Chief of Ordnance
Washington, D.C.

Sir

During the past week the only firing done has been with Warner's Breech Loading Carbine — which worked moderately well until the last round consisting of sixty-five (65) grains powder and seventeen hundred and fifty (1,750) grains lead.

On firing the gun this time the breech-piece was blown some ten feet into the air and the carbine rendered unserviceable. It is thought that this would not have occurred but for the bursting of the cartridge shell.

W.S. Smoot
Lt. of Ordnance

Washington Arsenal Tests

While this concluded testing of Warner's breechloader at the Springfield Armory, in November 1864, General Dyer requested Major Benton, Commander of the Washington Arsenal, undertake a trial of the Warner carbine using Spencer ammunition. The Spencer cartridge in use at this time, and for that matter used in all Spencer rifles and carbines during the Civil War was the No. 56 Navy and Infantry cartridge, otherwise known as the Spencer 56-56.[8]

REPORTS ON SMALL ARMS (CLASS 6)[9]

Report on Warners Carbine made by Maj. J.G. Benton Ordnance Dept. at Washington Arsenal 1864.

November 18, 1864

Gen'l. A.B. Dyer
Chief of Ordnance
Washington, D.C.

Sir:

Pursuant to your verbal instructions I have made a trial of Warner's carbine with the ammunition used in the Spencer carbine.

The Chamber of the former piece was reamed up from .52 in. to .564 in. in order that the cartridge of the latter might be inserted. The bore was not altered.

The result of the firing was very inferior to that ordinarily obtained and is shown in the accompanying record.

J.G. Benton
Maj. Ordnance

General Dyer was obviously not satisfied with the first test for in early December he gave Major Benton

EXPERIMENTS WITH SMALL ARMS, (Class 6.)

TARGET RECORD

Made at *Washington Arsenal*, by *J. C. Dudley Mr. Armr*, *Nov. 17*, 1864.

No. of Shots.	DISTANCES FROM CENTRE OF TARGET IN INCHES.				DISTANCES FROM CENTRE OF IMPACT IN INCHES.				MISSED.	REMARKS.
	VERTICAL.		HORIZONTAL.		VERTICAL.		HORIZONTAL.			
	Above.	Below.	Right.	Left.	Above.	Below.	Right.	Left.		
1	5		16			.7	26.7			Fired from shoulder
2		26		37		31.7		26.3		and rest
3	18		45		12.3		33.7			
4	37		28		31.3		38.7			Gun aimed five
5		Fell short								feet above centre of
6	22			5	16.3		5.7			target with rear
7		13	13			20.7	23.7			sight adjusted to
8	2			32		3.7		21.3		300 yards
9		24	40			29.7		29.3		
10		8	42			13.7		31.3		Chamber reamed
11	43		8		37.3		2.7			out to take cartridge
12	28		13		22.3			2.3		for Spencer Carbine
13		Fell short								
14	32		43		26.3		33.7			
15	9		19		3.3		28.7			
16		Fell short								
17	7		57		1.3			40.3		
18	4		47			1.7		36.3		
19		17	29			23.7		18.3		
20		19	43			25.7		32.3		
21										
22										
23										
24										
25										
	207	109	165	347	150.4	151.3	237.6	237.7		
	5.7		10.7		17.7		27.9			

Range: *300* Yards.
Gun: *Warner Carbine*
Diameter of bore: *.50* in
Length of barrel:
Weight:
Grooves, No. of:
  Do. Depth of:
  Do. Twist of:
Ammunition: } *Spencer Cartridge*
Ball, weight of: }
Powder, do. of: } *Diameter of ball .56 in*
Wind:

Jno. G. Dudley
Master Armorer

(B. & 11. 61. 2)
(O. O. No.)

EXPERIMENTS WITH SMALL ARMS, (Class 6.)

TARGET RECORD

Made at *Washington Arsenal*, by *Jno. G. Dudley*, *Dec. 1st*, 1864.

No. of Shots.	DISTANCES FROM CENTRE OF TARGET IN INCHES.				DISTANCES FROM CENTRE OF IMPACT IN INCHES.				MISSED.	REMARKS.
	VERTICAL.		HORIZONTAL.		VERTICAL.		HORIZONTAL.			
	Above.	Below.	Right.	Left.	Above.	Below.	Right.	Left.		
1	57		6		16.2			3.1		Fired from shoulder
2	33		40		13.2		27.9			and rest
3		11	10		31.8			2.1		
4		16	14		36.8		1.9			Gun aimed at center
5		18	12		38.8			1		of Target sighted or
6	55			0	34.2			12.1		rated per 300 yards
7	31		13		10.2			.9		
8	16		5			4.8		7.1		Chamber enlarged to
9	18		7			2.8		5.1		take the same cartridge
10	7		3		13.8			9.1		as Spencer's Carbine
11	45		15		24.2		2.9			
12	30		1		9.2			11.1		
13	30		13		9.2		.9			
14	25		7		4.2			5.1		
15		Fell short				Fell short				
16	46		21		25.2		8.9			
17	6		7		14.8			3.1		
18	55		6		34.2			6.1		
19		10	55		30.8		22.9			
20	18		13		2.8		.9			
21										
22										
23										
24										
25										Aver. 6 12.9
	452	55	231		179.0	177.2	66.2	66.1		
	20.8		12.1		15.7		6.9			

Range: *310* Yards.
Gun: *Warner's Carbine*
Diameter of bore:
Length of barrel:
Weight:
Grooves, No. of:
  Do. Depth of:
  Do. Twist of:
Ammunition: *Crittenden & Tibbals*
Ball, weight of:
Powder, do. of:
Wind:

Jno. G. Dudley
Master Armorer

(B. & 11. 61. 2)
(O. O. No.)

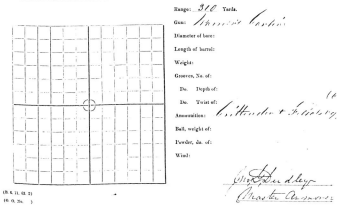

*Warner carbine target records dated November 17
and December 1, 1864.*   (National Archives)

orders to conduct a second test. Both tests were conducted, by J.G. Dudley, Master Armorer at the Washington Arsenal.

REPORT ON SMALL ARMS (CLASS 6)[10]

Report on Warner's Carbine made J.G. Benton Ordnance Department at Washington Arsenal 1864.

December 2nd, 1864

General A.B. Dyer
Chief of Ordnance
Washington, D.C.

Sir:

Pursuant to your verbal instructions I have made a further trial of the altered Warner Carbine with Spencer Carbine Cartridges.

By way of comparison, a Spencer Carbine was fired at the same time and under the same circumstances. The cartridges were one half Crittenden and Tibbals and one half Leets.

The results are shown in the accompanying target records and are herewith recapitulated as follows — viz.

Warner's Carbine

C & T Cartridges — Absolute 18.9"
Leets Cartridges — Absolute 24.7"

Spencer Carbine

C & T Cartridges — Absolute 13"
Leets Cartridges — Absolute 9.4"

It will be perceived that the Warner Carbine is much less accurate than the Spencer with the same kind of cartridges. I frequently observed considerable difficulty in extracting the case from the Warner Carbine and none in the Spencer.

I telegraphed Major Laidley some time ago for some Warner Carbine Cartridges, but have not yet received any. As soon as they arrive I will try them.

The Warner Carbine used in this trial was not the same one that was used in the trial report on the 18th ultimo.

J.G. Burton
Maj. Ord. Comdg.

P.S. Since writing the above I have ascertained that the sticking of the cartridge case was a consequence of the chamber being reamed out cylindrical. The fault is corrected by making the rear opening of the chamber one hundredth larger than the first.

Adoption of the Spencer Cartridge

As a result of these experiments the Ordnance Department must have felt that Warner's Carbine could be successfully altered to fire Spencer 56-56 cartridges.

Combined with reports that Crittenden & Tibbals could not produce both Spencer and Warner cartridges in the quantities, nor within the time period the government required,[11] must have prompted General Dyer to decide to offer Warner a second contract for 2,500 carbines, but this time requiring the arms be "reamed up so as to receive the cartridge now used in the Spencer Carbine."[12] It must have also been the reason for the decision to have the Washington Arsenal rechamber all the Warner carbines they currently had on hand to the Spencer cartridge. This amounted to approximately 550 guns, 500 of which would later be issued to the 3rd Massachusetts Cavalry.

The Laidley Ordnance Board - 1865

The Civil War had borne scores of different small arms, the majority of which required specialized ammunition. In an effort to resolve an obviously complex parts supply and ammunition problem General A.B. Dyer proposed to Secretary of War Stanton the following solution.[13]

Ordnance Office
December 5, 1864

Hon. E.M. Stanton
Secretary of War

Sir:

The experience of war has shown the breech loading arms are greatly superior to muzzle loaders for infantry, as well as for cavalry. Measure should immediately be taken to substitute a suitable breech loading musket, in place of the rifle musket which is now manufactured at the National armory and by private contractors for this department.

It is important that the best arm which is now made be adapted and that all breech-loaders thereafter made by or for this department shall conform strictly to it. No change shall be made until it shall have been clearly demonstrated that the change is a decided and important improvement.

With a view, therefore, to carry out these measures, I have the honor to request that a board, to be composed of ordnance, cavalry and infantry officers, be constituted to meet at Springfield Armory, and at such other place as the senior officer of the board may direct, to examine, test and recommend for adoptions a suitable repeater or magazine carbine. The arms recommended by the Board may, if approved by the War Department, be exclusively adopted for the military service.

A.B. Dyer
Chief of Ordnance

As a result carbine tests were ordered by the Secretary of War under Special Order 458. Accordingly, a board of officers convened at the Springfield Armory on January 4, 1865 for the purpose of examining, testing, and recommending for adoption a suitable breechloader for muskets and carbines and a repeater or magazine rifle. The arms they were to test are listed below.[14]

Allen & Brand Carbine & Rifle	Merrill Carbine
	Miller Carbine
Ball Carbine (repeater)	National Carbine & Rifle
Ballard Carbine & Rifle	Palmer Carbine
Beal Carbine	Peabody Carbine & Rifle
Berdan Rifle	Percy Carbine
Clark Carbine	Remington Carbine & Rifle
Cochran Carbine	Richardson Carbine & Rifle
Fields Carbine	Riche Carbine
Geiger Carbine	Root Carbine (Colt)
Goulding Carbine	Rowe Carbine
Gray Carbine (repeater) & Rifle	Sharps Carbine
	Smith Carbine
Green Carbine & Rifle	Snyder Carbine
Grillet Carbine	Spencer Carbine & Rifles (repeaters)
Gwyn Carbine (repeater)	
Gwyn & Campbell Carbine	Straw Carbine (single shot)
Hammond Carbine & Rifle	Straw Carbine (repeater)
Hayden (Wooden Model)	Starr Carbine
Hayden Rifle	Stevens Carbine & Rifle
Henry Rifle	Strong (repeater) (Wooden model)
Howe Carbine & Rifle	
Howard Carbine	Triplett & Scott Carbine
Jenks Carbine & Rifle	Walcott Carbine
Joslyn Carbine & Rifle	Warner Carbine
Laidley Carbine ("My Chick")	White Carbine & Rifle
	Wolcott Carbine
Landfear Carbine	Wright & Brown Carbine
Maynard Carbine	Yates (Wooden model)

Extracts of the board proceedings regarding Warner's carbine are as follows:[15]

> On January 9, 1865 the board met at 10 am. Mr. Warner of Springfield Massachusetts submitted a carbine which was fired one hundred times. Twenty shots were fired from it in one minute and forty-one seconds. Great difficulty was experienced in extracting some of the cartridge cases.
> On January 10, 1865 the board met at 10 am. Warner's carbine was examined by the board. Warner's carbine was again fired. One hundred shots were fired from it with very good results. Thirteen shots were fired in one minute.
> On March 24, 1865 the board met at 10 am. Guns already tested were divided into classes — those to be still further tested and those which required no further consideration."

Warners carbine was among the latter group!

Comments from the Field

The Journal of Accounts for Carbines examined at the Ordnance Office indicates that under Warner's first contract Colonel Thornton accepted delivery of 500 carbines at Warner's Springfield, Massachusetts facility on April 25, 1864. On June 23, 1864 Capt. R.A. Buffington is recorded to have received an additional 500 carbines at the New York Arsenal.[16]

Records of Ordnance Stores on hand at Armories, Arsenals & Depots indicates that on July 2, 1864 fifty Warners were on hand at the New York Arsenal and that by August 2, 1864 only two were available in New York but 548 were at the Washington D.C. Arsenal.[17]

It is concluded from this information that 450 of the first 500 Warners were issued to troops and that the second 500 arms plus 48 from the first lot went to Washington, while two remained at the New York Arsenal.

Summary statements of ordnance on hand in cavalry regiments during the 3rd Quarter ending September 1864 indicates the 1st Wisconsin Volunteer Cavalry Regiment, and more specifically probably Companies C and E located at Nashville, Tennessee where Warner Cartridges were being shipped, was armed with at least 200 Warner Carbines and 3,375 rounds of ammunition. Additionally the 1st Wisconsin had one Spencer and 142 Joslyn Carbines on hand.[18] During the same period a report on the Warner Carbine submitted by Lieutenants Charles S. Wicks, George Brown, James Crocker and Thomas Bateman all of the 1st Wisconsin Volunteer Cavalry stated that "these officers agree that they carry well, get out of order rather easily, (and) the stocks being of hard wood and brittle break most often. (They) prefer larger caliber and that they are good arms."[19]

On January 31st, 1865, a report was issued by Major David T. Bunker of the 3rd Massachusetts Cavalry concerning Warner carbines recently issued to his unit:[20]

> Headquarters 3rd Mass. Cavalry
> Remount Camp
> Pleasant Valley, MD
> Jan'y. 31, 1865

Major Elmer Otis
Special Inspector of Cavalry

Major:

> I have the honor to report results of a test of twenty six (26) Warner's Patent Carbines by Major Noyes, Capt. Stone and myself. The ammunition (Spencers) used was that drawn on requisition from Ordnance Officer. The pieces were loaded by Major Noyes, Capt. Stone and myself and notes taken. You

Left side of the Laidley Trials Warner carbine with breech block partially opened. The receiver is marked "James Warner, Springfield, Mass/Warners/Patent" in three lines, but lacks a serial number. Although the receiver is of a shorter design than the ones found on brass frame carbines, the barrel, extractor, rear sight and handguard appear to be standard production parts. The Laidley board photographed each trial gun both assembled and disassembled. The Iron Frame carbine submitted by Warner was 37-1/8 inches overall and weighed 6-1/4 pounds.

(Springfield Armory Museum Collection)

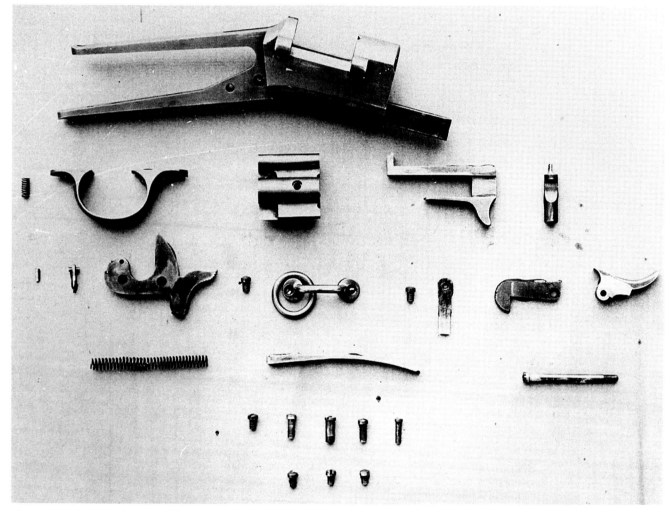

Component parts of the Laidley Trials Iron Frame Warner clearly illustrate a newly designed breech block locking mechanism, consisting of a flat-sided, curved end button which is checkered along its edge. Additionally, a standard sling bar and ring is mounted forward on the left side of the receiver.   (Springfield Armory Museum Collection)

will find the result of our observations in the accompanying Tabular Statement.

Cartridges marked "Pushed in with screwdriver" required considerable force to get them into the barrel.

Those marked "Plunger sticks" required a severe blow of the butt on a log to throw the plunger back so that the chamber could be opened.

In those marked "Chamber Stick" the chamber required a severe blow with a stick to open them after firing.

Those marked "Ejectors Slip" required the screw driver to remove the case after firing.

Those with "Chamber Blown Open" are for inspection in the condition they were in after firing.

Those marked "Stock Blown Off" had the stock which covers the spring of the ejector blown off.

Those marked "Breech Pin Broken" had breech pins broken by the recoil of pieces when discharged.

The accuracy with which these pieces can be fired is really astonishing. Our men who formally used "Sharps Old Carbine" can make as good shots with them as with Sharps and I should think with a great velocity.

After careful personal observation of these arms I am of the opinion that "Warners Patent Carbines" are entirely unfit for service in the field or elsewhere. In this I am seconded by Major E.S. Noyes and Capt. Chas Stone of my command.

Had time permitted I would have put them to a severer test and will do so yet if you deem it advisable.

I have the honor to herewith submit a number of reports from company commanders of tests made by them.

David T. Bunker
Major, Comdg. Regt.

No. of Carb. Used	No. of Rounds Fired	Cart. pushed in with screw driver	Non explosions	Plunger sticks	Chamber would not open or sticks	Ejector slips
26	520 in all of the carbines 20 discharges to each piece	47	64	48	162	50

Chamber Blown Open	Breech Pin Broken		Stocks Blown Off
5	1		1

Attached to his report Major Bunker enclosed reports of his company commanders. They were:

Lieutenant H. P. Brownwell	Company A
Lieutenant A. D. Elliott	Company B
Lieutenant P. S. Curry	Company C

Lieutenant H. P. Hughes	Company D
Lieutenant M. McDonald	Company E
Captain F. E. Frothingham	Company F
Lieutenant F. Campbell	Company G
Lieutenant R. P. Granger	Company H
Lieutenant J. F. Simonds	Company I

Four days later Major Bunker again wrote to Major Otis submitting an addition to his January 31st. report.[21]

> Hd. Qrs. 3rd Mass. Cavalry
> Remount Camp, MD
> February 3rd, 1865

Major Elmer Otis
Special Inspector of Cavalry
Middle Military Division

Major

I have the honor to submit the following addition to my report of a "test" of 26 "Warners Patent Carbines". Of these 26, seven were rendered unserviceable after firing of rounds indicated below.

Williams — Chamber blown open after firing four rounds.

Goodrich — Chamber blown open after firing six rounds.

Stevens — Chamber blown open after firing first round.

Eddy — Chamber blown open after firing first round.

Mower — Chamber blown open after firing first round.

Creddock — Chamber blown open after firing first round.

Harmon — Chamber blown open after firing first round.

David T. Bunker
Major 3rd Mass. Cav.

Problems Confirmed

As a result of Major Bunker's reports, Major Benton, Commander of the Washington Arsenal, dispatched master armorer J.G. Dudley to the field for a first-hand evaluation of the problem with the Warner arms. One of the reasons for Dudley's selection could possibly have been that he was the armorer who supervised the modification and conducted the tests of Warner carbines to accept the Spencer cartridge on November 17 and December 1st, 1864. A telegram sent by First Lieutenant McKee at Harpers Ferry to the Chief of Ordnance on December 6th, 1864, asks "Have the Warner Carbines at the Washington Arsenal been reamed up and if so to please send them to the Harpers Ferry depot."[22] This evidence would indicate that the

Washington Arsenal was, in fact, rechambering the nearly 550 Warner Carbines they had on hand at that time to accept the Spencer 56-56 cartridge. Since the Warners issued to the 3rd Massachusetts were chambered to receive the "Spencer and Joslyn cartridge" (56-56 Spencer) it is reasonable to assume that 500 of the Warner Carbines recently rechambered at the Washington Arsenal were, in fact, those weapons that Major Benton referred to in his report.[23]

J.G. Dudley's report read as follows:

REPORTS ON SMALL ARMS (CLASS 6)

Report on Warner Carbine made by J.G. Dudley Master Armorer at Washington Arsenal 1865.

February 20, 1865

Major J.G. Benton
Comdg. Arsenal

Sir

Agreeably to your order dated 15th instant I have examined the Warner carbines issued to the 3rd Regt. Mass. Cavalry at Camp Pleasant Valley, VA and respectfully submit the following report.

Twenty-five carbines were selected from the whole number in the hands of the Regt. and 20 shots from each piece fired at random with the cartridges the Regt. have on hand (Crittenden & Tribbals). Many of the cases burst in firing causing the igniting pin to stick and not work free, from the escape of gas which prevented the cap piece from being thrown up with the thumb and finger.

The slot in the cap-piece in which the catch works, became considerably widened in some of the guns which prevented the cap piece form being held down well in its place by the latch.

Nearly all of the carbines can be pulled off at half cock — some require but a slight pull to bring the hammer down.

Thirty two carbines were found to be unserviceable — two with stocks broken, the others with screws broken and the cap-piece hinge joint screw badly strained.

But one carbine was found that would not eject the case easily, the cause of that one working badly seemed to be in consequence of the gun being snapped without a cartridge case in the chamber. The igniting pin had stuck on the edge of the chamber of the barrel forcing the metal inward, forming a slight burr on the inside chamber.

A carbine (new) taken from this arsenal was fired with the Crittenden & Tribbals cartridges. Several cases burst which caused the igniting pin to stick and prevent the cap piece from being thrown up.

Some cartridges taken from this arsenal made by Leet, Springfield Mass., about 80 were fired, but one case burst. The guns worked much better with this cartridge.

I respectfully call your attention to what seems to be the principal defects in the gun.

The igniting pin is liable to stick and not work free, especially when cases burst and gas escapes. The pin would work much better had it a spring to force it back when relieved from the pressure of the hammer.

The escape of gas from cartridge cases bursting (caused by being made of inferior or thin copper) is liable to strain and widen the slot in the cap-piece giving the catch too much play.

The hammer may ignite a cartridge by being pulled off at half cock.

To carry a gun using ammunition of this kind with the hammer full down on the cartridge is I believe considered unsafe.

J.G. Dudley
Master Armorer

P.S. The cartridges the above Regt. have on hand were made by Crittenden & Tibbals and are not reliable. Many of them contained no fulminate, as they failed to ignite after repeated trials.

The copper from which the cartridge cases are made is very inferior in quality. In some the case would burst at the point where the igniting pin struck it, and in others the head burst entirely out.

Upon receipt Major Benton added the following endorsement and forwarded it to Brig. General Dyer.[24]

Respectfully forwarded to the Chief of Ordnance for his information. From the liability of the arms to get out of order by the sticking of the igniting pin arising from foulness, I think it would be well to withdraw them from the hands of the troops and replace them by some more reliable weapons.

J.G. Benton
Major, Ordnance

General Dyer, in turn, forwarded the report to Colonel Thornton, Inspector of Contract Arms at New York, and also sent a copy to James Warner.[25]

Ordnance Office
War Department
Washington, DC - Feb. 22nd, 1865

Mr. James Warner
Springfield, Mass.

Sir

The enclosed copy of a report made by Mr. J.G. Dudley, Master Armorer, Washington Arsenal is communicated for your information. The reports from the field have been so bad relative to these arms that Mr. Dudley was sent to make a special trial, the result of which confirms all the bad reports previously received.

A.B. Dyer
Brig. Gen. Chief of Ordnance

Warner's decision not to incorporate a firing pin spring, as clearly evidenced in his drawings for patent #41,732, in favor of the beveled grooves on the barrel and frame claimed in patent #45,660, had come back to haunt him.[26] General Dyer's involvement must have prompted questions as to who was responsible for the problem at Remount Camp, even though the principal cause of the problem was the faulty ammunition supplied by Crittenden & Tibbals.

In an effort to avoid blame, Lieutenant McKee sent the following letter:[27]

Headquarters, Middle Military Division
Office, Chief of Ordnance Officer
Winchester, VA — March 1st, 1865

Brig. General A.B. Dyer
Chief of Ordnance
Washington, D.C.

General:

I have the honor to state that four hundred and ninety three (493) Warners Carbines have been condemned by an armorer sent from Washington to inspect them, and I would respectfully state further that Major E. Otis, Special Inspector of Cavalry is responsible for the dead loss to the Government in the transportation of these carbines from Washington. He went in person to the Ordnance War Department and made arrangements to have them reamed up and informed me that General Dyer had ordered the carbines to be put in order and at his request I sent a telegram to the Ordnance Office, December 6, 1864, inquiring whether they had been reamed up and requesting them to be sent to Harpers Ferry, VA Depot. I would regret exceedingly to be held responsible for Major E. Otis' selection of ordnance and ordnance stores, and would respectfully state that there is no telling what confusion and pecuniary loss to the Government may result if he be allowed to make arrangements for carbines etc. to be sent to depots under my charge. I will not therefore order these carbines back to Washington Arsenal until I receive instructions from you to that effect.

Geo W. McKee
Lt. & Chief of Ordnance Officer
Mid Mil Division

The following day, General Dyer received a telegram from Major Otis:[28]

Office U.S. Military Telegraph
War Department

The following telegraph received at Washington, 2 pm, March 2, 1865 from Harpers Ferry, March 2, 1965.

B. General Dyer
Chief Ordnance

There are four hundred and ninety three (493) Warner's Carbines here in the hands of Lt. Hoyt, acting Ordnance Officer, Remount Camp. Shall I order them to Washington, D.C. Arsenal? Seven (7) have already been sent. Lt. McKee declines to order them back as he did not order them here.

Elmer Otis
Major 1st. U.S. Cavalry
Special Inspector

Reasons for Warner carbines being withdrawn from service were not entirely due to design deficiencies. The ammunition issued to the 3rd Massachusetts Cavalry was definitely part of the problem. Cartridges cases either failed to fire or when they did, often ruptured, thus preventing extraction. Or worse, some would blow open the breech, endangering the shooter.

Maintaining a spring-loaded firing pin in production arms could have prevented the problem of jammed breeches when firing pins penetrated and subsequently stuck inside the cartridges. However, being able to fire the arm while the hammer was at half-cock was a definite safety hazard.

The combination of all of these problems, coupled with the fact that the war was almost over, must have been part of the reason for the government's eventual decision to withdraw the 500 Warner Carbines issued to the 3rd Massachusetts Cavalry. What eventually happened to these arms is unknown. However, in the March 1865 report of Small Arms in the Hands of Troops, the Military Division of the Mississippi indicated that within its 1st, 2nd, 4th and 5th Cavalry Divisions 361 Warner carbines were still in service.[29] These were probably the original weapons issued to the 1st Wisconsin Cavalry in the summer of 1864, and still chambered for the original Warner cartridge.

Standard Warner production model carbine, Serial No. 474, modified with a Greene model type breech block locking mechanism and rechambered for the wartime 56-56 Spencer cartridge. The original Warner model breech block locking mechanism (the "flipper") has been permanently fixed with an additional screw and the spring below the flipper has been removed. The flipper has been reshaped to the contour of the receiver. The breech block has a small brass piece pinned into the slot the flipper used to enter to hold the breech block in position. In addition, the left side of the breech block has been milled to accept Greene model breech block parts. Although the barrel of the carbine is "CSL" proofed, it is unclear whether this modification was a U.S. Government arsenal experiment, or civilian modification.   (Author's Collection)

CHAPTER 6

POST WAR SALES

The Final Days

Warner completed the last deliveries of his carbines on March 15, 1865. In total, he had provided 4,001 carbines from both his Springfield factory and that of his subcontractor, the Greene Rifle Works at Worcester, Massachusetts.

By then, however, the war was almost over. On April 9th, General Lee surrendered his Army of Northern Virginia to General Grant at Appomatox Court House. Two weeks later, on April 26, near Raleigh, North Carolina, General Johnson, upon receiving word of Lees action, surrendered his army to General Sherman at Durham Station.[1]

Although the final surrender of confederate troops would not occur until May 26th, it was clear that the end of the war was imminent. Accordingly, on April 28th, the War Department issued an order to cease further purchase of war supplies:[2]

General Orders	War Department
No. 77	Adjutant General
	Washington — April 28, 1865

For reducing expenses of the Military Establishment Ordered.

I. That the chiefs of the respective bureaus of this Department proceed immediately to reduce of their respective departments to what is absolutely necessary, in view of an immediate reduction of the forces in the field and garrison and the speedy termination of hostilities, and that they severally make out statements of the reductions they deem practicable.

IV. That the Chief of Ordnance stop all purchase of arms, ammunition and materials therefore, and reduce the manufacturing of arms and ordnance stores in the Government arsenals as rapidly as can be done without injury to the service.

W.A. Nichols
Assistant Adjutant General

Carbine Production

Five years of conflict had prompted the federal government to purchase almost 2 million muskets and rifles, and more than 400 thousand cavalry carbines. On October 26, 1866, Brevet Major-General A.B. Dyer, Chief of Ordnance, provided a summary statement of weapons and associated munitions that had been purchased by the government between January 1, 1861 and June 30, 1866.[3] The purchase of carbines and ammunition alone was substantial.

Class 6

Carbines

1,509	Ballard	$35,140.00
1,002	Ball	25,387.00
55,567	Burnside	1,412,620.41
9,342	Cosmopolitan	199,838.29
22,728	Gallager	508,492.94
1,052	Gibbs	27,995.25
3,520	Hall	64,763.50
11,261	Joslyn	282,586.00
892	Lindner	19,895.00
14,495	Merrill	374,804.63
20,202	Maynard	489,399.78
1,001	Palmer	20,918.50
20,000	Remington	436,752.00
80,512	Sharps	2,213,192.00
30,062	Smith	745,645.24
94,196	Spencer	2,393,633.82
25,603	Starr	586,773.79
4,001	Warner	79,310.54
151	Wesson	3,491.75
200	French Carbines	4,800.00
10,051	Foreign Carbines	66,193.00
587	Musketoons	5,815.50
407,934		$9,997,448.94

Class 8

Cartridges

3,527,450	Ballard	$57,945.05
21,819,200	Burnside	547,490.05
6,300,000	Cosmopolitan	132,007.27
8,294,023	Gallager	211,893.92
173,760	Green	3,869.82
4,610,400	Henry	107,353.00
515,416	Joslyn	12,953.37
100,000	Lindner	2,262.00
2,157,000	Maynard	72,207.50
5,502,750	Merrill	105.779.32
4,257,000	Remington	68,600.00
16,306,508	Sharps	347,410.57
1,001,000	Sharps & Hankins	27,402.00
13,861,500	Smith	377,569.78

58,238,924	Spencer	1,419,277.16
6,860,000	Starr	140,768.30
1,028,000	Warner	27,472.00
46,409,514	Rifle, Cal .58	712,913.05
254,000	Wesson	3,666.60
6,021,220	Buck & Ball	86,982.28
842,880	Le Faucheux	17,039.00
2,735,180	Round Ball	51,273.12
2,047,011	Blank	10,153.05
2,852,000	Carbine	63,227.38
26,225,930	Pistol	390,485.86
10,000	Gardener's Shell	350.00
241,950,666		$4,998,333.51

Disposition of Arms

Following the cessation of hostilities, it quickly became evident to the government that they were now faced with a vast surplus of arms and equipment of all types. General Dyer's grand total of all the ordnance stores purchased during the course of hostilities came to a sizable $130,266,364.79.[4] In an effort to recoup some of this expense, ordnance agencies, arsenals and depots were given authority to sell at auction much of their surplus and unserviceable equipment. Registers of Ordnance stores sold between 1868 and 1875 indicate that Warner carbines and ammunition were among the contents of some of these sales.[5]

April 1868 — U.S. Ord. Agency, N.Y. City by BVT
Col. S. Crispin
1 Warner Carbine — Condition New to Baker
& Co. — $10.00
63 Warner Carbines — Cal .50 to C.H. Pond
@ $8.50 each
(1st Class Condition)
97 Warner Carbines — Cal .50 to C.H. Pond
@ $6.50 each
(2nd Class Condition)
10 Boxes, Packing @ $1.00 to C.H. Pond
48,000 Warner Cartridges @ $18.00/1,000 to
C.H. Pond

August 1868 — Augusta Arsenal, GA by
BVT LTC D.W. Flagler
1 Warner Carbine-Serviceable Cal .50 to
Baker & Co. @ $15.00

June 2, 1869 — St. Louis Arsenal, Mo. by
BVT Brig Gen. G.D. Ramsay
49 Warner Carbines — Condition Burnt to
J.P. Moorer & Son @ $4.90 each.

April 1869 — St. Louis Arsenal, Mo. by
BVT Brig. Gen. F.D. Callender
50 Warner Carbines to Mr. Folsom @ $.50 each.

March 1869 — St. Louis Arsenal, Mo. by BVT
Brig. Gen. F.D. Callendar
10 Warner Carbines to D. Lippincott @ $4.50 ea.

November 1870 — New York Agency by Major S.
Crispin
2492 Warner Carbines Cal .50 New to
Schuyler, Hartley & Graham @
$12.35 ea. (includes 2492 Barrel
wipers, thongs and screw drivers in
155 arms chests).
925,372 Ball cartridges for Warners Carbine
new in 911 boxes @ $16.00 per box
to Schuyler, Hartley & Graham.

August 10, 1871 — Frankford Arsenal, PA by
Major T.J. Treadwell.
3 Warners Cal .50 to J. Thorp @ $2.25 ea.

October 4, 1871 — Leavenworth Arsenal KA by
Capt. A. Meordecai
9 Warners to Heamer Fisher @ $1.00 ea.

July 17, 1872 — New York Agency by Major S. Crispin
1 Warner Cal .50 to Abram S. Hipewitt
condition unseen @ $8.50.

April 1873 — New York Agency by Major S. Crispin
Scrap metal being spare arms parts
containing 2 1/16 pounds of Warner
parts in serviceable condition — (no
buyer named).

June 16, 1974 — New York Agency by Lt. J.G. Butler
449 Warner Carbine cartridge boxes @ $.05
1/4 ea. to John P. Moore & Son.
Total paid $23.57.

June 1875 — New York Agency by Lt. J.G. Butler
3 boxes of Warner cartridges (40 rounds) in a
lot sale with other cartridges. (No
buyer named).

Between 1868 and 1870 major arms manufacturers such as Colt and E. Remington & Sons, as well the large arms dealerships of Schuyler, Hartley & Graham, Herman Boker, and Austin Baldwin & Co. successfully bid on substantial quantities of U.S. government surplus arms.[6] With the threat of a Franco-Prussian War (1870-1871) about to turn into reality, there is little doubt that some, if not all of the arms they purchased at auction were intended for export to France.

Sales to France

The 2,492 Warners sold to Schuyler, Hartley & Graham, together with 21,117 Remingtons, 338 percussion Smiths, 6,000 Amoskeg-marked Lindners, 6,000 Joslyns, 2,500 metallic cartridge Gallagers, 2,742 Spencers, and 432 Sharps carbines and an unspecified amount of ammunition were delivered to France in 1870. However upon their arrival it was found that the Warners, Joslyns, Gallagers and Spencers were chambered for the Civil War era Spencer 56-56 cartridge, while the ammunition purchased was the later (and smaller) Spencer 56-50 cartridge.

The confusion that probably ensued must have driven the decision to retain in the French arsenals at Lyon, LaRochelle and Bayonne, all the carbines except the Remington .50 caliber split-breech carbine, which were already chambered for the 56-50 cartridge. Following the close of hostilities, 2487 Warners, together with the other carbines that had been kept in storage, and "3,677,182 ill-assorted cartridges" were sold for a very low price at public auction at the Bayonne arsenal on April 21, 1871.[7]

Standard design of packing box for carbines and muskets. Prior to 1865, carbines were packed twenty to a box. In early 1865, however, carbines were delivered ten to a box. This reproduction from photographs and drawings of originals boxes is designed to contain ten Warner carbines. An appendage well, large enough to pack five brushes, cleaning thongs and screwdrivers, was located at each end of the box. (Author's Collection)

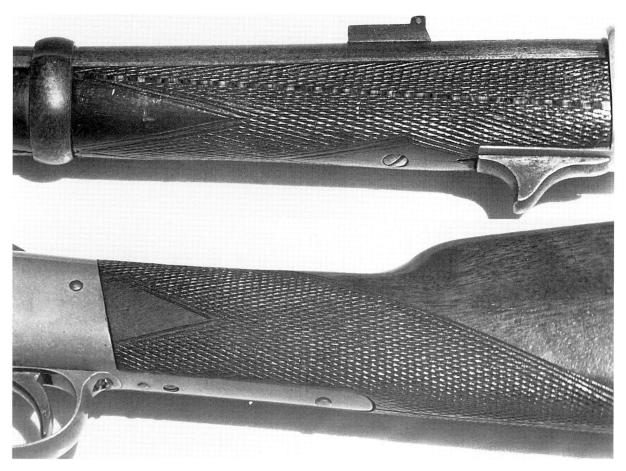

Checkering often found on Greene model carbines with English proof marks. This suggests these carbines were exported to England and probably checkered to increase their appeal for sale on the civilian market. (Author's Collection)

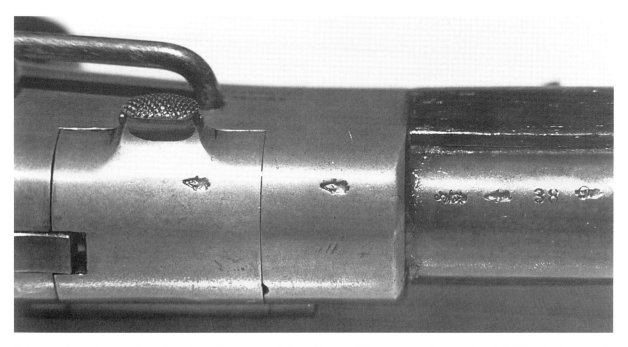

English proof marks are often found on Greene model carbines. "Crown over intertwined G&P" is the proof mark and "Crown over V" is the view mark for the Worshipful Company of Gunmakers of the City of London; 38 denotes bore size (.50 cal); an unknown proof mark is located on the barrel immediately ahead of the receiver. (Author's Collection)

EPILOGUE

Following the end of the American Civil War, things probably became progressively worse for both Emery and Warner. The "Greene Rifle Works, manufacturers of Greene Breech Loading percussion rifles and carbines" is last listed in the Worcester City Directory of 1867.

Warner's Springfield operations ended that same year. In order to pay off the Scrugham notes, Warner mortgaged $12,000 for his business in March 1866.[1] However, with no further government contracts and little demand for his carbine on the civilian market, he was eventually forced to sell his business to Charles T. Grilley of New Haven, Connecticut on April 30, 1867, for a mere $10,900.[2]

The Longmeadow Road factory was eventually sold to the Havermeyer Paper Mache Company. The Havermeyer family, in turn, deeded the factory and its property in 1892 to the City of Springfield to permit expansion of Forest Park. Shortly thereafter, the factory was dismantled and torn down.[3]

With his percussion pistol designs now obsolete, cartridge pistol patents unlawful to produce, breechloading carbine sales to the government terminated, and loss of his factory, James Warner must have found it increasingly difficult to justify remaining in Springfield. Accordingly, in 1868 he moved his family to Manatee County, Florida and established a homestead on a tract of land along the Manatee River just south of present day Tampa.[4] One year after his arrival to begin a new life in Florida, he died on October 11, 1869.[5]

Longmeadow Road factory site c. 1890s, following demolition to enlarge Forest Park.

(Connecticut Valley Historical Museum)

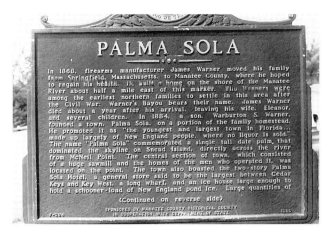

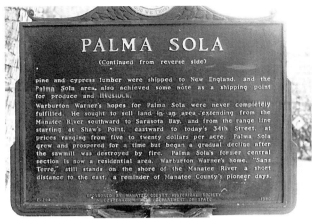

A roadside marker located near the mouth of Warner's Bayou in Palma Sola, Florida.

(Right)   Grave marker of James and Eleanor Warner, Fogartyville Cemetery, Palma Sola, Florida.

Joe Warner and Marian (Warner) Bates, great-grandchildren of James Warner.

Appendix A

JOURNAL OF ACCOUNTS — CARBINES

Journal of Account for (James Warner) Carbines examined at the Ordnance Office and Transmitted to the Second Auditor for settlement.

Payment Date	No. Carb.	Price Each	Total	Cases	Total Amount Paid	Delivery Location	Delivery Date
Jan. 24, 1864	1[1]	$18.00	$18.00	—	$18.00	Washington	
May 14, 1864	500	$18.00	$9,000.00	$ 87.50	$ 9,087.50	Springfield	Apr. 25, 1864
July 28, 1864	500	$18.00	$9,000.00	$ 87.50	$ 9,087.50	N.Y. Arsenal[2]	June 23, 1864
Dec. 7, 1864	500	$20.00	$10,000.00	$ 87.50	$10,087.50	Springfield	Nov. 15, 1864
Feb. 18, 1865	500	$20.00	$10,000.00	$ 87.50	$10,087.50	Springfield	Feb. 2, 1865
Feb. 27, 1865	500	$20.00	$10,000.00	$150.00	$10,150.00	Worcester	Feb. 18, 1865
Mar. 6, 1865	800	$20.00	$16,000.00	$160.00	$16,160.00	Springfield	Feb. 27, 1865
Apr. 14, 1865	700	$20.00	$14,000.00	$632.54[3]	$14,632.54	Worcester	Mar. 15, 1865
TOTAL	4001				$79,310.54		

Authors Notes
Note 1: Pattern Model Carbine Serial No. 94 sent to the Ordnance Office
Note 2: Warner Model Carbines forwarded to Capt. Buffington, N.Y. Arsenal
Note 3: Costs for drilling vent holes, cases, etc.

References
NA RG 156 Entry 164, Vol. 7, 8, 9.

APPENDIX B

REGISTER OF MANUFACTURERS — CARBINES

Register of Manufacturers of Carbines or parties applying for orders to fabricate the same or who have such stores for sale.

Date of Application	Name	Residence	Address	Kind of Stores	Number	Each	Remarks
Feb. 29, 1864	Greene's Rifle Works	Worcester Mass.	Wash. D.C.	Warner's Carbines	2,500		
Apr. 27, 1864	James Warner	Springfield Mass.	—	Warner's Carbines	50,000		
Nov. 16, 1864	Greene's Rifle Works	New York Carbines	—	Warner's	3,000		20-50 per day. Price same as price paid James Warner
Nov. 17, 1864	James Warner	Springfield Mass.	—	Warner's Carbines	10 or 15,000	$22	First delivery 3 mos. from date of contract
Oct. 30, 1865	Greene's Rifle Works	Boston Mass.[1]	39 State Street	Warner's Carbines	1,800	$20	

Authors Note
Note 1: Of the 3000 carbines the Greene Rifle Works produced, only 1200 were sold to the government. These must have been the 1800 remaining carbines.

Reference
NA RG 156 Entry 85, Vol. II.

APPENDIX C

JOURNAL OF ACCOUNTS — CARTRIDGES

Journal of account for (James Warner) Carbine Cartridges examined at the Ordnance Office and transmitted to the Second Auditor for settlement.

Payment Date	No. Carb.	Price Each	Total	Cases	Total Amount Paid	Delivery Location	Delivery Date
June 11, 1864	9,000[1]	$25.00	$ 225.00	$ 4.50	$ 229.50	N.Y. Agency	May 9, 1864
Sept. 9, 1864	100,000[2]	$26.00	$2,600.00	$ 59.25	$2,659.25	N.Y. Agency	Aug. 30, 1864
Dec. 2, 1864	120,000[3]	$26.00	$3,120.00	$ 90.00	$3,210.00	N.Y. Agency	Nov. 22, 1864
Jan. 12, 1865	150,000[4]	$26.00	$3,900.00	$112.50	$4,012.50	N.Y. Agency	Dec. 31, 1864
Feb. 9, 1865	300,000	$26.00	$7,800.00	$225.00	$8,025.00	N.Y. Agency	Feb. 3, 1865
Mar. 7, 1865	349,000	$26.00	$9,074.00	$261.75	$9,335.75	N.Y. Agency	Feb. 24, 1865
	1,028,000				$27,472.00		

Authors Notes
Note 1: Delivery by Warner, but probably manufactured by C.D. Leet
Note 2: This and all subsequent deliveries by C.D. Leet
Note 3: 90,000 rounds subsequently shipped from N.Y. to Nashville, Tenn.
Note 4: 110,000 rounds subsequently shipped from N.Y. to Nashville, Tenn.

Reference
NA RG 156 Entry 164, Vol. 7, 8, 9.

APPENDIX D

REGISTER OF MANUFACTURERS — CARTRIDGES

Register of Manufacturers of Powder, Cartridges and Caps or of parties applying for orders to fabricate the same or who have such stores for sale.

Date of Application	Name	Residence	Kind of Stores	Number	Price/m	Remarks
Apr. 13, 1864	James Warner	Springfield Mass.	Warner's Carbine Cartridges	—	$25	Construction
Apr. 27, 1864	James Warner	Springfield Mass.	Warner's Carbine Cartridges	10,000	$25	
May 9, 1864	D.C. Sage	Middleton Conn.	Warner's Carbine Cartridges	—	$26	25,000/day from July 1, 1864
June 30, 1864	C.D. Leet	Springfield Mass.	Warner's Carbine Cartridges	1,000,000	$26	

Reference
NA RG 156 Entry 85, Vol. II.

APPENDIX E

RECORDS OF WARNER CARBINES IN THE FIELD

September 1, 1864 —
Department of Cumberland at Atlanta, Georgia. 7,193 Carbines: Spencers, Merrills, Sharps, Burnsides, Warners. Also 45 Gallagers and 837 Smiths in 1, 2, 3, & 4 Divisions, Cavalry Corps.[1]

September 30, 1864 —
1st Wisconsin Cavalry Regiment. Carbines: 1 Spencer, 142 Joslyn, 200 Warner, 1,000 Joslyn cartridges and 3,375 Warner cartridges.[2]

October 1, 1864 —
Department of Cumberland at Atlanta, Georgia. 5,031 Carbines: Spencers, Merrills, Sharps, Burnsides, Warners. Also 259 Gallagers, Smiths and Maynards in 1, 2, 3 & 4 Divisions, Cavalry Corps.[3]

November 1, 1864 —
Chattanooga, Tennessee. 673 Carbines: Spencers, Merrills, Sharps, Burnsides, Warners, Gallagers, Smiths in Cavalry Corps.[4]

February 1, 1865 —
Military Division of the Mississippi. (Report from Nashville, Tennessee). 1,189 Spencer, 614 Sharps, 1,009 Burnside, 4 Maynard, 343 Warner, 145 Smith in 1st Division, Cavalry Corps.[5]

March 1, 1865 —
Military Division of the Mississippi (Report from Nashville, Tennessee). 76 Ballard (Cal. 42), 908 Burnsides, 74 Gallagers, 6 Joslyns, 488 Maynards, 1,473 Sharps, 154 Smiths, 8,629 Spencers, 378 Starrs, 361 Warners in 1, 2, 4 & 5 Divisions, Cavalry Corps.[6]

References
  Note 1, 3, 4: NA RG 156 E-21 Box 229
  Note 5, 6: NA RG 156 E-21 Box 242
  Note 2: NA RG 156 E-110 Microfilm Roll 3

APPENDIX F

Component parts of the Warner Breech Loading Carbine with price of each part.

Springfield, January 17, 1865

1	Lock Frame	$5.00	22	Stirrup	.10
2	Lock Frame Tang Screw	.02	23	Stirrup Rivet	.01
3	Lock Frame Cap	.25	24	Guard	.50
4	Lock Frame Screw	.02	25	Guard Screws (2)	.04
5	Breech Block	.65	26	Sling Ring	.12
6	Breech Block Joint Screw	.02	27	Sling Ring Bolt	.20
7	Breech Block Catch	.25	28	Sling Ring Bolt Nut	.08
8	Breech Block Catch Screw	.02	29	Barrel	1.50
9	Breech Block Catch Spring	.02	30	Front Sight	.25
10	Breech Block Plunger	.25	31	Rear Sight Base	.35
11	Breech Block Plunger Screw	.02	32	Rear Sight Base Screw	.04
12	Hammer and Tumbler (in one piece)	.70	33	Rear Sight Leaf	.20
13	Hammer and Tumbler screw	.02	34	Rear Sight Leaf Joint Screw	.02
14	Sear and Trigger (in one piece)	.30	35	Band	.30
15	Sear and Trigger screw	.02	36	Band Spring	.10
16	Sear and Trigger Spring	.10	37	Stock	1.60
17	Sear and Trigger Spring Screw	.02	38	Stock Tip or Forearm	.15
18	Cartridge Extractor	.50	39	Stock Tip Screw	.02
19	Cartridge Spring	.05	40	Stock Tip Screw Washer	.02
20	Main Spring	.25	41	Butt Plate	.30
21	Main Spring Strain Screw	.02	42	Butt Plate Screws (2)	.04

TOTAL $14.44

Reference
NA RG 156 Entry 21, Box 235

APPENDIX G

WARNER'S PATENTS

UNITED STATES PATENT OFFICE.

JAMES WARNER, OF SPRINGFIELD, MASSACHUSETTS.

IMPROVEMENT IN BREECH-LOADING FIRE-ARMS.

Specification forming part of Letters Patent No. **41,732,** dated February 23, 1864.

To all whom it may concern:

Be it known that I, JAMES WARNER, of Springfield, in the county of Hampden and State of Massachusetts, have invented a new and useful Improvement in Breech-Loading Fire-Arms; and I do hereby declare that the following is a full, clear, and exact description of the same, reference being had to the accompanying drawings, forming part of this specification, in which—

Figure 1 is a central longitudinal section of the frame, the breech, and part of the barrel of a fire-arm with my improvement. Fig. 2 is a transverse section of the frame and breech. Fig. 3 is a top view corresponding with Fig. 1.

Similar letters of reference indicate corresponding parts in the several figures.

This invention relates to that construction of breech-loading fire-arms in which the breech opens with a swinging movement about an axis situated at one side of the frame and parallel with the bore of the barrel.

It consists, first, in a novel construction of such breech, and of that part of the frame of the "arm" which receives it, whereby, while the strength of the frame is retained in the greatest possible degree, great convenience is afforded for loading with fixed ammunition. In order to provide for the firing, the breech is fitted—like the breeches of some other breech-loading arms—with a sliding pin, upon which the hammer strikes to drive it against that portion of the shell of the ammunition which contains the priming; and a second feature of the invention consists in a certain arrangement and combination of the said sliding pin, the hammer, and a recess in the back of the breech, whereby, when the breech is closed and the hammer down, the hammer is made to lock the breech securely.

To enable others skilled in the art to make and use my invention, I will proceed to describe its construction and operation.

A is the frame of the arm, having the barrel B screwed into it at *a a*, and having the chamber within the barrel, the rear end of which is countersunk, as shown at *b b*, to receive the flange *c* of the shell C of the fixed ammunition. D is the breech, connected by a hinge-joint, *d d*, with the right side of the frame, the axis of the said hinge being parallel with the bore of the barrel. This breech closes into an opening, *e e' f g g*, in the frame, and its back and

the back of the said opening are made slightly taper toward the bottom, as shown at *e'* in Fig. 1, in order that the breech may close tightly, but open without friction. The said opening is long enough to receive the fixed ammunition. The bottom *f* of the said opening is made of a semi-cylindrical form, and of a width sufficient to receive the flanged portion of the shell of the fixed ammunition, and it is parallel to the bore of the barrel, as shown in Fig. 2, so as to be equivalent to a continuation of the lower part of the chamber. Above the semi-cylindrical bottom *f* the said opening extends all across the frame, as shown at *g g* in Fig. 2. The breech is made to fit the opening in the frame having at its bottom a semi-cylindrical projection, *h*, which fits snugly into the semi-cylindrical bottom of said opening, and having shoulders *p p* on each side to fit the parts *g g* of the said opening, and its exterior conforms to the upper part of the frame A, so that when closed it is flush therewith. By this construction of the frame and breech peculiar facility is afforded for loading, as the bottom *f* of the opening forms a channel to guide the ammunition into the chamber of the gun, and the frame is not unnecessarily weakened, as it would be by making the bottom of the opening of larger size, as is the case in many other fire-arms, and the breech fitting to said opening is held very firmly in its place.

E is the hammer arranged within the frame in rear of the breech, and operated in the usual manner.

F is the sliding pin inserted through a hole in the breech to be struck by the hammer, and thereby driven forward against the flange of the shell C to explode the fulminate priming and fire the charge. This pin has applied to it a spiral spring, *j*, Fig. 1, to draw it back within the breech, and a stop-screw, *k*, to prevent it from being drawn back by the spring farther than is necessary. The said pin is made shorter than the breech, and a recess, *l*, wide and deep enough for the reception of the hammer, is provided in the rear end of the breech for the hammer to enter to strike the said pin for the purpose of firing the arm, and this recess also constitutes the means of locking the breech in a closed condition by means of the nose of the hammer, for the hammer, when let down while the breech is closed, is permitted by the shortness of the pin F to enter

2 ...·   ,   **41,732**

the said recess, and so prevent the possibility of moving the breech sidewise until it (the hammer) has been pulled back.

G is a slide for withdrawing the discharged shells of the ammunition from the chamber, working through a groove, *n*, in the frame, operated by means of a trigger, H, and moved forward again by a spring, *m*, after the shell has been withdrawn and the trigger has been liberated.

I do not claim, broadly, the invention or use of a hinged breech; but

What I claim as my invention, and desire to secure by Letters Patent, is—

The construction of the semi-cylindrical recess *f*, of a diameter corresponding to that of the flange of the metallic cartridge, in combination with the semi-cylindrical breech-piece projection *h*, the recess *l*, and the hammer E, as herein shown and described, so that when the breech-piece is open the cartridge-case will be guided in an exact line with the barrel, both in loading and withdrawing the case, and when the breech-piece is closed the solid portion thereof or semi-cylindrical projection will press against the rear of the cartridge-shell, while the fall of the hammer will lock the breech-piece, and prevent it from being blown open by the accidental rearward bursting of the shell, the premature discharge or striking of the hammer upon the cartridge-pin being also avoided, all as set forth.

JAMES WARNER.

Witnesses:
   M. M. LIVINGSTON,
   HENRY MORRIS.

United States Patent Office.

JAMES WARNER, OF SPRINGFIELD, MASSACHUSETTS.

IMPROVEMENT IN BREECH-LOADING FIRE-ARMS.

Specification forming part of Letters Patent No. **45,660,** dated December 27, 1864; antedated December 14, 1864.

To all whom it may concern:

Be it known that I, JAMES WARNER, of Springfield, in the county of Hampden and State of Massachusetts, have invented certain new and useful Improvements in Breech-Loading Fire-Arms; and I do hereby declare that the following is a full, clear, and exact description of the same, reference being had to the accompanying drawings, forming a part of this specification, in which—

Figure 1 is a side view of the breech part of a fire-arm with my improvements. Fig. 2 is a central longitudinal vertical sectional view of the same. Fig. 3 is a top view of the same. Fig. 4 is a transverse vertical sectional view of the same immediately in front of the breech-piece, looking toward the barrel.

Similar letters of reference indicate corresponding parts in the several figures.

This invention consists in certain novel means of producing the extraction of a pin which works through such a breech-block as is above mentioned for the purpose of being struck by the hammer to fire the charge, whereby the necessity for a spring in combination with the said pin is obviated.

To enable others skilled in the art to make and use my invention, I will proceed to describe its construction and operation.

A is the frame of the arm, having the barrel B screwed into it in the usual manner, and having a suitable cavity, $a\,a\,b\,b$, in the rear of the barrel for the reception of the solid movable breech-block C, which opens and closes the rear end of the barrel by a swinging movement upon a pin or hinge, c, situated on the right side of the frame. On the left-hand side of this breech-block is a thumb-piece, d, to which to apply the thumb of the left hand to start it from the cavity $a\,a\,b\,b$, if necessary, for the purpose of opening the chamber of the barrel for loading.

D is the locking device for locking the breech-block in the closed position, consisting of a lever fitted to work in a mortise, e, which is cut in the frame A, parallel with and on the left-hand side of the mortise f, in which the hammer E works. This lever works on a fulcrum-pin, g, which is inserted through the slot, and it has applied under it, within the mortise f and in rear of the fulcrum-pin, a spring, h, which always tends to press upward its rear end, and thereby cause its front end to enter a notch, i, in the rear end of the breech-block when the latter is closed, and so lock the said block in the closed position. The rear end of the said lever projects upward in such a manner that after firing the operator may, without relinquishing the grasp of his right hand, first half-cock the hammer and then apply his thumb to press down the said end of the lever, by which means the front end of the said lever is drawn out of the notch i and the breech-block unlocked. By turning the arm over quickly on its right side the breech-block will then usually fall open to permit the loading, the pressure of the left thumb against the thumb-piece d being only necessary in case of the breech-block sticking. When the breech-block is swung back into the cavity $a\,a\,b\,b$ to close the chamber after loading, it presses against the rounded upper portion of the front of the lever D, and so presses it back until the block arrives in the proper position, when the lever is thrown into the notch i by the spring h. The facility with which the breech-block can be unlocked by merely shifting the thumb from the hammer to the lever D simplifies the operation of reloading and enables the repetition of the fire to be performed very rapidly.

F is the sliding pin working through the breech-block, for the hammer to strike upon to effect the ignition of the charge. The movement of the pin is limited to what is necessary by means of a screw, j, which is screwed into the breech-piece transversely to the said pin, and the point of which enters a notch or groove, k, in the said pin. The said pin has no spring applied to it, but is permitted to move back and forth with perfect freedom. In order that it may not interfere with the opening and closing movements of the breech-block, its front end is rounded, and in the upper part of the rear end of the barrel there is a beveled groove, l, and in the part of the frame C above the said end of the barrel a beveled groove, m, (see Figs. 2 and 4,) the said grooves being so arranged that the end of the pin F may work in them. In the opening movement of the breech-block, the rounded front end of the pin, passing up the bevel of the groove l, causes the pin to be forced back flush with the front face of the breech-block, and in the closing movement of the breech-block the said rounded end, if it

2   45,660

protrudes through the front face of the said block, is pushed back flush with the said face by passing down the bevel of the groove m. The necessity of the spring is thus dispensed with, and the number of the parts of the arm and the liability to get out of order thereby reduced.

G is the cartridge-shell extractor, of common construction, consisting of a slide arranged below the barrel, and having a turned-up lip, n, at its rear end to enter a recess, o, in the lower part of the rear end of the barrel, as shown in Fig. 2, the said lip being formed to fit the cartridge-shells. The slide G is furnished below the barrel with a handle, p, by which to draw it back by hand for the purpose of extracting the shells after firing, and it has applied to it a spring, q, to push it forward again after the extraction of the shell, and preparatory to reloading. To provide a firm bearing directly under the extractor while it is in position for firing, and also during the whole of its backward movement, so that it may support and prevent the explosion of that portion of the flange of the cartridge-shell which is received within it, and also be prevented from slipping past the flange in the act of withdrawing the shell, I provide in the frame A, in the rea

the barrel and at the bottom of the cavity a a b b, a mortise, r, which is just wide and deep enough for the slide G to work in, the said mortise being continued through that portion of the frame immediately under the barrel. The rear end of the slide, which has the tip n upon it, rests upon the solid flat bottom of this mortise, both at the time of firing and during the act of extracting, and thus has at all times as firm a bearing as though it were a solid portion of the barrel or frame of the arm. In order that the extractor may not be prevented from coming back to its proper place by any accumulation of dirt between the lip n and the barrel, the front of the recess o in the barrel is beveled in a downward direction to form a space for the dirt to work into, as shown in Fig. 2.

What I claim as my invention, and desire to secure by Letters Patent, is—

The beveled grooves l and m in the barrel and frame, in combination with the sliding pin F, substantially as and for the purpose herein specified.

JAMES WARNER.

Witnesses:
WM. L. SMITH,
WM. S. SHURTLEFF.

ENDNOTES

PROLOGUE

1. Fogartyville Cemetery marker, Bradenton, Florida.
2. Marion W. Bates, unpublished paper, "The life of Eleanor Scrugham Warner," Feb. 16, 1976.
3. Marion W. Bates, great granddaughter, personal interview of family history.
4. Lee Arbuckle, "The 'Other' Springfield,"*The Gun Report*, September 1987.
5. Connecticut Historical Society, Sam'l Colts Own Records, 1949, 80.
6. Bates, note 2.
7. *Ibid.*
8. J. Thomas Scharf, "History of Westchester County New York", 1886.
9. Bates, note 2.
10. Springfield City Clerks records, 1850.
11. Connecticut Historical Museum, Local History Department, letter dated July 12, 1988; Source Registry and Deeds for Hamden County, multiple entries 1850-1870.
12. US Federal Census Return, 1860.
13. Marius B. Paladeau, "Springfield Arms Co. Revolvers," *The American Rifleman*, Feb. 1967, n. 4.
14. Springfield City Directory, 1851-52.
15. *Ibid.*
16. Connecticut Valley Historical Museum, Local History Department, letter dated July 12, 1988; Source Hamden County Registry of Deeds.
17. Paladeau, n. 13.
18. Connecticut Valley Historical Museum, letter dated July 12, 1988.
19. Paladeau, n. 13.
20. Connecticut Valley Historical Museum, letter dated July 12, 1988; Source Registry of Deeds for Hamden County, 1862-66.
21. Pamphlet, Springfield Department of Parks and Recreation, "Pecousic Villa, Home of the late Everett H. Barney," n.d.
22. Franklin P. Rice, *Dictionary of Worchester Mass* Blanchard and Co., 1893.
23. Andrew F. Lustyik, "Joslyn: The Man and His Carbines," *The American Rifleman*, July 1868.
24. Greene letter, February 21, 1864, (National Archives and Records Administration, Record Group 156, *Records of the Office of the Chief of Ordnance)*. Hereafter cited as NARA, RG 156.
25. Warner letter, February 27, 1864, (NARA, RG 156).

CHAPTER 1: PATENTS

1. Case history file, Patent No. 41,732, (National Archives and Records Administration, Record Group 241, *Patent Office Records)*. Hereafter cited as, NARA, RG 241.
2. *Ibid.*

3. *Ibid.*
4. *Ibid.*
5. *Ibid.*
6. *Ibid.*
7. *Ibid.*
8. *Ibid.*
9. *Ibid.*
10. Case history file, Patent No. 45,660, (NARA, RG 241).
11. *Ibid.*
12. *Ibid.*
13. *Ibid.*

CHAPTER 3: GOVERNMENT CONTRACTS

1. Brig. Gen. James W. Ripley to James Warner, Apr. 25, 1863, "Letters, Endorsements, and Reports Sent" (NARA, RG 156).
2. Brig. Gen. James W. Ripley to James Warner, May 8, 1863, "Letters, Endorsements, and Reports Sent" (NARA, RG 156).
3. Brig. Gen. James W. Ripley to James Warner, May 22, 1863, "Letters, Endorsements, and Reports Sent" (NARA, RG 156).
4. James Warner to Gen. James W. Ripley, July 6, 1863, "Letters Received," (NARA, RG 156).
5. Brig. Gen. James W. Ripley to James Warner, Oct. 27, 1863, "Letters, Endorsements, and Reports Sent" (NARA, RG 156).
6. Lt. Col. P. V. Hagner to Gen. G. D. Ramsay, Nov. 16, 1863, "Letters Received," (NARA, RG 156).
7. Lt. Col. P. V. Hagner to Gen. G. D. Ramsay, Dec. 28, 1863, "Letters Received," (NARA, RG 156).
8. Ledger entry of a letter from James Warner, Dec. 31, 1863, "Letters Received," (NARA, RG 156).
9. Gen. G. D. Ramsay to Col. W. A. Thornton, Jan. 2, 1864, "Letters, Telegrams, and Endorsements Sent" (NARA, RG 156).
10. Brig. Gen. G. D. Ramsay to James Warner, Jan. 7, 1864, "Letters, Endorsements, and Reports Sent" (NARA, RG 156).
11. Brig. Gen. G. D. Ramsay to Col. W. A. Thornton, Jan. 7, 1864, "Letters, Telegrams, and Endorsements Sent" (NARA, RG 156).
12. James Warner to Brig. Gen. G. D. Ramsay, Jan. 8, 1864, "Letters Received," (NARA, RG 156).
13. Brig. Gen. G. D. Ramsay to James Warner, Jan. 11, 1864, "Letters, Telegrams, and Endorsements Sent" (NARA, RG 156).
14. Brig. Gen. G. D. Ramsay to James Warner, Jan. 20, 1864, "Letters, Telegrams, and Endorsements Sent" (NARA, RG 156).
15. Brig. Gen. G. D. Ramsay to James Warner, Feb. 15, 1864, "Letters, Telegrams, and Endorsements Sent" (NARA, RG 156).
16. James Warner to Brig. Gen. G. D. Ramsay, Feb. 27, 1864, "Correspondence and Reports Relative to Inspection of Ordnance," (NARA, RG 156).
17. Capt. G. T. Balch to Col. W. A. Thornton, Feb. 27, 1864, "Letters, Telegrams, and Endorsements Sent" (NARA, RG 156).

18. James Warner to Brig. Gen. G. D. Ramsay, Feb. 29, 1864, "Correspondence and Reports Relative to Inspection of Ordnance," (NARA, RG 156).
19. Capt. G. T. Balch to James Warner, Mar. 1, 1864, "Letters Received," (NARA, RG 156).
20. Capt. G. T. Balch to Col. W. A. Thornton, Mar. 1, 1864, "Letters Received," (NARA, RG 156).
21. Col. W. A. Thornton to Brig. Gen. G. D. Ramsay, Mar. 8, 1864, "Letters Received," (NARA, RG 156).
22. Col. W. A. Thornton to Brig. Gen. G. D. Ramsay, Mar. 19, 1864, "Reports of Experiments," (NARA, RG 156).
23. James Warner to Brig. Gen. G. D. Ramsay, Apr. 5, 1864, "Letters Received," (NARA, RG 156).
24. Col. W. A. Thornton to Brig. Gen. G. D. Ramsay, Apr. 8, 1864, "Letters Received," (NARA, RG 156).
25. Capt. G. T. Balch to James Warner, Apr. 25, 1864, "Letters, Endorsements, and Reports Sent" (NARA, RG 156).
26. Capt. G. T. Balch to Col. W. A. Thornton, Apr. 22, 1864, "Letters, Telegrams, and Endorsements Sent" (NARA, RG 156).
27. James Warner to Secretary of War, Apr. 29, 1864, "Press Copies of Letters and Endorsements Sent to the Secretary Of War," (NARA, RG 156).
28. Brig. Gen. G. D. Ramsay to James Warner, Apr. 29, 1864, "Register of Communications Referred to the Secretary of War," (NARA, RG 156).
29. Brig. Gen. G. D. Ramsay to James Warner, Apr. 29, 1864, "Letters, Telegrams, and Endorsements Sent" (NARA, RG 156).
30. Col. W. A. Thornton to Brig. Gen. G. D. Ramsay, May 5, 1864, "Letters Received," (NARA, RG 156).
31. James Warner to Brig. Gen. G. D. Ramsay, May 6, 1864, "Letters Received," (NARA, RG 156).
32. James Warner to Brig. Gen. G. D. Ramsay, May 7, 1864, "Letters Received," (NARA, RG 156).
33. Brig. Gen. G. D. Ramsay to Col. W. A. Thornton, May 10, 1864, "Letters, Telegrams, and Endorsements Sent" (NARA, RG 156).
34. Brig. Gen. G. D. Ramsay to James Warner, May 10, 1864, "Letters, Telegrams, and Endorsements Sent Relative to the Manufacture, Procurement, and Repair of Ordnance Supplies and Equipment," (NARA, RG 156).
35. James Warner to Capt. G. T. Balch, May 19, 1864, "Correspondence and Reports Relative to the Inspection of Ordnance," (NARA, RG 156).
36. Brig. Gen. G. D. Ramsay to James Warner, May 20, 1864, "Letters, Endorsements, and Circulars Sent" (NARA, RG 156).
37. Brig. Gen. G. D. Ramsay to Col. W. A. Thornton, May 20, 1864, "Letters Received," (NARA, RG 156).
38. James Warner to Brig. Gen. G. D. Ramsay, June 11, 1864, "Correspondence and Reports Relative to Inspection of Ordnance," (NARA, RG 156).
39. Brig. Gen. G. D. Ramsay to James Warner, June 20, 1864, "Letters, Endorsements, and Circulars Sent" (NARA, RG 156).
40. Brig. Gen. G. D. Ramsay to James Warner, June 27, 1864, "Letters, Endorsements, and Circulars Sent" (NARA, RG 156).
41. James Warner to Brig. Gen. G. D. Ramsay, June 29, 1864, "Letters Received," (NARA, RG 156).
42. Gen. G. D. Ramsay to Col. W. A. Thornton, June 30, 1864, "Letters, Telegrams, and Endorsements Sent to Ordnance Officers and Military Storekeepers," (NARA, RG 156).
43. James Warner to Brig. Gen. G. D. Ramsay, June 30, 1864, "Letters Received," (NARA, RG 156).
44. Col. W. A. Thornton to Brig. Gen. G. D. Ramsay, July 2, 1864, "Letters Received," (NARA, RG 156).
45. James Warner to Brig. Gen. A. B. Dyer, Oct. 22, 1864, "Letters Received," (NARA, RG 156).
46. Brig. Gen. A. B. Dyer to Col. W. A. Thornton, Nov. 11, 1864, "Letters Received," (NARA, RG 156).
47. Col. W. A. Thornton to Capt. A. R. Buffington, Nov. 12, 1864, "Letters Received," (NARA, RG 156).
48. James Warner to Brig. Gen. A. B. Dyer, Oct. 29, 1864, "Letters Received," (NARA, RG 156).
49. Brig. Gen. A. B. Dyer to Jamer Warner, Nov. 4, 1864, "Letters, Endorsements, and Circulars Sent" (NARA, RG 156).
50. James Warner to Brig. Gen. A. B. Dyer, Nov. 8, 1864, "Letters Received," (NARA, RG 156).
51. James Warner to Col. W. A. Thornton, Nov. 15, 1864, "Receipts of Orders and Contracts," (NARA, RG 156).
52. James Warner to Brig. Gen. A. B. Dyer, Nov. 17, 1864, "Register of Letters Received," (NARA, RG 156).
53. James Warner to Brig. Gen. A. B. Dyer, Nov. 16, 1864, "Letters Received," (NARA, RG 156).
54. James Warner Application to Army Ordnance Dept., Nov. 17, 1864, "Register of Applications for Orders from Manufacturers and Suppliers of Ordnance," (NARA, RG 156).
55. James Warner to Brig. Gen. A. B. Dyer, Nov. 22, 1864, "Letters Received," (NARA, RG 156).
56. James Warner to Brig. Gen. A. B. Dyer, Nov. 28, 1864, "Letters Received," (NARA, RG 156).
57. Brig. Gen. A. B. Dyer to Col. W. A. Thornton, Nov. 30, 1864, "Letters, Telegrams, and Endorsements Sent to Ordnance Officers and Military Storekeepers," (NARA, RG 156).
58. Col. W. A. Thornton to Brig. Gen. A. B. Dyer, Dec. 1, 1864, "Letters Received," (NARA, RG 156).
59. Brig. Gen. A. B. Dyer to James Warner, Dec. 3, 1864, "Letters, Endorsements, and Circulars Sent" (NARA, RG 156).
60. Brig. Gen. A. B. Dyer to Col. W. A. Thornton, Dec. 3, 1864, "Letters, Telegrams, and Endorsements Sent to Ordnance Officers and Military Storekeepers," (NARA, RG 156).
61. James Warner to Brig. Gen. A. B. Dyer, Dec. 5, 1864, "Letters Received," (NARA, RG 156).
62. Brig. Gen. A. B. Dyer to Col. W. A. Thornton, Dec. 7, 1864, "Letters, Telegrams, and Endorsements Sent to Ordnance Officers and Military Storekeepers," (NARA, RG 156).
63. Brig. Gen. A. B. Dyer to James Warner, Dec. 7, 1864, "Letters, Endorsements, and Circulars Sent" (NARA, RG 156).
64. James W. Emery to Brig. Gen. A. B. Dyer, Dec. 7, 1864, "Letters Received," (NARA, RG 156).
65. James Warner to Brig. Gen. A. B. Dyer, Dec. 19, 1864, "Letters Received," (NARA, RG 156).
66. Brig. Gen. A. B. Dyer to Honorable Edwin M. Stanton, Dec. 31, 1864. "Press Copies of Letters and Endorsements Sent to the Secretary of War," (NARA, RG 156).
67. James Warner to Brig. Gen. A. B. Dyer, Jan. 7, 1865, "Letters Received," (NARA, RG 156).
68. Brig. Gen. A. B. Dyer to James Warner, Jan. 10, 1865, "Letters, Endorsements, and Circulars Sent" (NARA, RG 156).
69. Brig. Gen. A. B. Dyer to Col. W. A. Thornton, Jan. 10, 1865, "Letters, Telegrams, and Endorsements Sent to Ordnance Officers and Military Storekeepers," (NARA, RG 156).
70. Journal of Accounts for Carbines—Account of James Warner, "Receipts of Orders and Contracts," (NARA, RG 156).
71. Brig. Gen. A. B. Dyer to Col. W. A. Thornton, Mar. 3, 1865, "Letters, Telegrams, and Endorsements Sent to Ordnance

Officers and Military Storekeepers," (NARA, RG 156).

72. Registers of Manufactures of Carbines or of Parties Applying for Orders to Fabricate the Same or Who Have Such Stores for Sale," Account of James Warner, (NARA, RG 156).

CHAPTER 4: AMMUNITION

1. Col. W. A. Thornton to Brig. Gen. G. D. Ramsay, Mar. 8, 1864, "Letters Received," (NARA, RG 156).
2. James Warner to Secretary of War, Apr. 27, 1864, "Registers of Communications Referred to the Secretary of War," (NARA, RG 156).
3. James Warner to Brig. Gen. G. D. Ramsay, May 7, 1864, "Letters Received," (NARA, RG 156).
4. C. D. Leet to Brig. Gen. G. D. Ramsay, Apr. 22, 1864, "Letters Received," (NARA, RG 156).
5. C. D. Leet to Brig. Gen. G. D. Ramsay, July 7, 1864, "Letters Received," (NARA, RG 156).
6. C. D. Leet to Brig. Gen. G. D. Ramsay, Aug. 16, 1864, "Letters Received," (NARA, RG 156).
7. C. D. Leet to Brig. Gen. G. D. Ramsay, Sept. 16, 1864, "Letters Received," (NARA, RG 156).
8. Proceedings of the Ordnance Board Convened in Washington, D.C. Under Special Order 410, Sept. 16, 1863, "Registers of Letters Received by the Inspection Division," (NARA, RG 156).
9. Capt. Crispin to Brig. Gen. A. B. Dyer, Dec. 16, 1864, "Letters Received," (NARA, RG 156).
10. Roy M. Marcot, *Spencer Repeating Firearms* (Irvine, CA: Northwood Heritage Press, 1983), 197.

CHAPTER 5: TEST AND EVALUATION

1. Maj. A. B. Dyer to Brig. Gen. G. D. Ramsay, Mar. 8, 1864, "Experiments: Registers of Correspondence and Reports of Experiments," (NARA, RG 156).
2. Maj. A. B. Dyer to Brig. Gen. G. D. Ramsay, Apr. 16, 1864, "Reports of Experiments," (NARA, RG 156).
3. Maj. A. B. Dyer to Brig. Gen. G. D. Ramsay, May 28, 1864, "Reports of Experiments," (NARA, RG 156).
4. Service Record of A. B. Dyer—1864, "Military Service History of Ordnance Officers," (NARA, RG 156).
5. Lt. W. S. Smoot to Brig. Gen. A. B. Dyer, Sept. 19, 1864, "Reports of Tests of Ordnance and Proceedings of Boards Making Tests," (NARA, RG 156).
6. Lt. W. S. Smoot to Brig. Gen. A. B. Dyer, Sept. 26, 1864, "Reports of Tests or Ordnance and Proceedings of Boards Making Tests," (NARA, RG 156).
7. Lt. W. S. Smoot to Brig. Gen. A. B. Dyer, Oct. 5, 1864, "Reports of Tests of Ordnance and Proceedings of Boards Making Tests," (NARA, RG 156).
8. Marcot, *Spencer Repeating Firearms*, 186.
9. Maj. J. G. Benton to Brig. Gen. A. B. Dyer, Nov. 18, 1864, "Reports of Experiments," (NARA, RG 156).
10. Maj. J. G. Benton to Brig. Gen. A. B. Dyer, Dec. 2, 1864, "Reports of Experiments," (NARA, RG 156).
11. Capt. Crispin to Brig. Gen. A. B. Dyer, Dec. 16, 1864, "Letters Received," (NARA, RG 156).
12. Brig. Gen. A. B. Dyer to James Warner, Dec. 7, 1864, "Letters, Endorsements, and Circulars Sent," (NARA, RG 156).
13. Marcot, *Spencer Repeating Firearms*, 100.
14. Secretary of War Special Order #458, Jan. 4, 1865, "Reports and Correspondence of Ordnance Boards," (NARA, RG 156).

15. Report on Warner Carbine, Jan. 9, 1865, "Reports and Correspondence of Ordnance Boards," (NARA, RG 156).
16. Journal Entries, May 14, 1864 and July 28, 1864, "Receipts of Orders and Contract," (NARA, RG 156).
17. Journal Entries Re: Warner Carbines on Hand, "Summary Statement of Ordnance and Ordnance Stores on Hand at Armories, Arsenals, and Depots," (NARA, RG 156).
18. Journal Entries Re: Warner Carbines and Ammunition on Hand, 3rd Quarter ending Sept. 1864, "Quarterly Summary Statement of Ordnance and Ordnance Stores in Hands of Regular Army and Volunteer Cavalry Regiments," (NARA, RG 156).
19. Journal Entry: 1st Wisconsin Volunteer Cavalry Regiment report on Warner Carbines — 3rd Quarter 1864, "Officers Reports on Small Arms," (NARA, RG 156).
20. Maj. D. T. Bunker to Maj. Elmer Otis, Jan. 31, 1865, "Reports of Experiments," (NARA, RG 156).
21. Maj. D. T. Bunker to Maj. Elmer Otis, Feb. 3, 1865, "Reports of Experiments," (NARA, RG 156).
22. Lt. G. M. McKee to Brig. Gen. A. B. Dyer, Dec. 6, 1865, "Letters Received," (NARA, RG 156).
23. J. G. Dudley to Maj. J. G. Benton, Feb. 20, 1865, "Reports of Experiments," (NARA, RG 156).
24. J. G. Dudley to Maj. J. G. Benton, Feb. 20, 1865, "Reports of Experiments," (NARA, RG 156).
25. Brig. Gen. A. B. Dyer to Col. W. A. Thornton, Feb. 22, 1865, "Letters, Endorsements, and Circulars Sent," (NARA, RG 156).
26. Patent #41732 and #45660 — Warner Breechloaders, "Patent Drawings and Correspondence," (NARA, RG 241—Warner Breechloading Firearms).
27. Lt. G. M. McKee to Brig. Gen. A. B. Dyer, March 1, 1865, "Reports of Experiments," (NARA, RG 156).
28. Maj. Elmer Otis to Brig. Gen. A. B. Dyer, March 2, 1865, "Reports of Experiments," (NARA, RG 156).
29. Journal Entry Re: Warner Carbines: Monthly Report of Field Artillery and Small Arms in the Military Division of the Mississippi O/A 1 March 1865, "Letters Received," (NARA, RG 156).

CHAPTER 6: POST WAR SALES

1. Rossiter Johnson, *Campfires and Battlefields* (NY: The Civil War Press,1967), 446.
2. Marcot, 91.
3. Claud E. Fuller, *The Rifled Musket* (NY: Bonanza Books, 1958), 260-262.
4. *Ibid.*, 262.
5. National Archives, Record Group 156, Entry 124, Book 4, Numerous entries.
6. William B. Edwards, *Civil War Guns* (Harrisburg, PA: The Stackpole Company, 1962), 407.
7. Pierre Lorain, *Les Armes Americaines de la Defense Nationale, 1870-1871* (Paris, France: 1970), 70.

EPILOGUE

1. Registry of Deeds for Hampden County, Mass., 1866.
2. *Ibid.*
3. Municipal Register of the City of Springfield for 1893.
4. Warner, James. *The Singing River* (1986), 19.
5. Bradenton, Florida, Fogartyville Cemetery marker.

BIBLIOGRAPHY

PRIMARY SOURCES

Bates, Marian W. *The Life of Eleanor Scrugham Warner*, Feb. 1976.

Connecticut Valley Historical Museum Local History Department, Correspondence, 1988.

National Archives of the United States
Record Group 156: Records of the Office of the Chief of Ordnance

Entry 3. Letters, Endorsements and Circulars Sent

Entry 5. Endorsements and Reports sent to Sec'y. of War

Entry 6. Letters, Telegrams and Endorsements sent to Ordnance Officers and Military Storekeepers

Entry 8. Press copies of letters and endorsements sent to Secretary of War

Entry 10. Register of Communications referred to Sec'y of War

Entry 13. Letters, Telegrams and Endorsements Sent relative to Manufacture, Procurement, Repair of Ordnance Supplies and Equipment.

Entry 20. Register of Letters Received.

Entry 21. Letters Received.

Entry 79. Statements of Purchases of Ordnance

Entry 80. Ledgers of Receipts in Connection with Orders and Contracts for Ordnance

Entry 81. Registers of Contracts and Orders of Ordnance

Entry 83. Statements of Purchases Under Contracts Exceeding $1,000

Entry 85. Registers of Applications for Orders from Manufacturers and Suppliers of Ordnance

Entry 103. Summary Statement of Ordnance and Ordnance Stores on hand at Armories, Arsenals and Depots.

Entry 110. Quarterly Summary Statement of Ordnance and Ordnance Stores in hands of Regular Army and Vol. Cavalry Regiments.

Entry 124. Abstracts of Reports of Sales of Ordnance Stores at Depots and Arsenals.

Entry 125. Journals of Ordnance Store Sales at Arsenals and Depots.

Entry 152. Statement of Accounts for Contractors

Entry 164. Receipts of Orders and Contracts

Entry 176. Military Service History of Ordnance Officers

Entry 193. Registers of Letters Received Relative to Improvements and Inventions.

Entry 199. Experiments: Registers of Correspondence and Reports on Experiments.

Entry 201. Reports of Experiments.

Entry 215. Officers Reports on Small Arms.

Entry 232. Ordnance Board Records 1864-1865.

Entry 323. Registers of Letters Received by Inspection Division.

Entry 994. Correspondence Relating to Inventions.

Entry 1006. Correspondence and Reports Relative to Inspections of Ordnance.

Entry 1012. Reports and Correspondence of Ordnance Boards.

Entry 1351. Letters sent by Springfield Armory

Entry 1356. Reports of Tests of Ordnance and Proceedings of Boards Making Tests.

Still Photograph Branch-Breech Loading Small Arms Photographs.

Record Group 217: General Accounting Office Records.

Entry 233. Ordnance Contracts

Record Group 241: Patent Office Records
Patent Correspondence Office, Washington National Records Center, Suitland, Maryland.
Patent Drawings, National Archives' Cartographic and Architectural Branch, Alexandria, Virginia.

Patent and Trademark Office, Patent Section, Crystal City Plaza, Washington, D.C.

Registry of Deeds for Hamden County, Mass. 1866.

Registry, Municipal of the City of Springfield, Mass., 1893.

Reilly, Robert M. *United States Military Small Arms 1816-1865*, Eagle Press Inc. Baton Rouge, Louisiana, 1970.

Rice, Franklin P., *Dictionary of Worcester and its Vicinity*, Blanchard & Co., 1893.

Scharf, J. Thomas. *History of Westchester County New York*, Philadelphia, Pennsylvania, 1886.

Smithsonian Institute, *Museum of American History and Technology Weapons Collection*, Washington, D.C.

Springfield Department of Parks and Recreation, *Pecousic Villa - Home of the Late Evert H. Barney*, Connecticut Valley Historical Museum, Springfield, Mass.

Springfield City Directory, numerous entries. Connecticut Valley Historical Museum, Springfield, Mass.

Springfield Armory Museum Weapons Collection, Springfield, Mass.

United States Military Academy Museum Weapons Collection, West Point, N.Y.

Secondary Sources

Arbuckle, Lee, The "Other" Springfield, *The Gun Report*, September 1987.

Barney, G.M., *Everett Hosmer Barney*, Springfield, Mass., 1912.

Connecticut Historical Society, *Sam'l Colts Own Records*, 1949.

Edwards, William B., *Civil War Guns*, The Stackpole Co., Harrisburg, PA, 1962.

Fuller, Claud E., *The Breech Loader in the Service*, Flayderman & Co., New Milford, Conn., 1965.

Fuller, Claud E., *The Rifle Musket*, Bonanza Books, New York, 1958.

Gluckman, Arcadi, *U.S. Muskets, Rifles and Carbines*, The Stackpole Co., Harrisburg, PA, 1959.

Hoyem, George A., *The History and Development of Small Arms Ammunition*, Armory Publications, Tacoma, WA., 1981.

Howard, Robert, *The Warner Carbine*, American Society of Arms Collectors Paper, October 1981.

Johnson, Rossiter, *Campfires and Battlefields*, The Civil War Press, N.Y., 1967.

Lindsay, Merrill, *The New England Gun*, Worcester Mass. City Library.

Lorain, Pierre, *Les Armes Americianes de la Defense Nationale 1870-1871*, Paris, France, 1970.

Lustyik, Andrew F., "Joslyn: The Man and His Carbines," *The American Rifleman*, Washington, D.C., July 1968.

Lustyik, Andrew F., "The Warner Carbine," *World Wide Gun Report*, Aledo, IL, May 1960.

Lustyik Andrew F., "Civil War Carbines," *World Wide Gun Report*, Aledo, IL, 1962.

Marcot, Roy M., *Spencer Repeating Firearms*, Northwood Heritage Press, Irvine, CA., 1983.

NRA Collectors Guide, National Rifle Association, Washington, D.C., 1972.

Peladeau, Marius B., "Springfield Arms Co. Revolvers," *The American Rifleman*, Washington, D.C., February 1967.

Scientific American Magazine, Library of Congress, Washington, D.C., Vol. 10, 12.

U.S. Federal *Census*, 1860.

Warner, James, *The Singing River*, 1986.

Wright, Harry A., *The Story of Western Massachusetts*, Lewis Historical Publishing Co., N.Y.

ABOUT THE AUTHOR

Alan Hassell was born on Staten Island, New York in 1944. He earned his bachelor's degree in geology from Alleghney College in Meadville, Pennsylvania. Subsequently, he completed a Master's degree and four additional post graduate degrees.

He entered the United States Air Force in 1966 and graduated from pilot school the following year. He has had assignments to Spain, England, Germany and South Vietnam, as well as numerous locations in the United States.

During his twenty-six year military career, he logged over 6600 hours flying various models of the C-130 aircraft and flew 139 long-range combat rescue missions in Southeast Asia. His decorations include the Defense Superior Service Medal, the Distinguished Flying Cross and eight Air Medals.

After retiring at the rank of Colonel from the USAF, he became the assistant general manager of a building materials store. He currently resides with his wife in Shalimar, Florida.

THOMAS BOOKS ON RELATED TOPICS

Civil War Guns
by William B. Edwards

Civil War Sharps Carbines & Rifles
by Jerry Coates & John McAulay

Introduction to Civil War Small Arms
by Jerry Coates & Dean Thomas

The Pitman Notes on U.S. Martial Small Arms and Ammunition, 1776-1933
by Brig. Gen. John Pitman (5 volumes)

Ready, Aim, Fire... Small Arms Ammunition in the Battle of Gettysburg
by Dean Thomas

A Handbook of Civil War Bullets and Cartridges
by Jim Thomas & Dean Thomas

Round Ball to Rimfire, A History of Civil War Small Arms Ammunition, Part One
by Dean Thomas

The Rimfire Cartridge in the United States and Canada
by John Barber

A History of Modern U.S. Military Small Arms Ammunition, Vol. 1 (revised)
by F.W. Hackley, W.H. Woodin, and E.L. Scranton

Small Arms 1856, Reports of Experiments with Small Arms for the Military Service
by U.S. Ordnance Department

THOMAS PUBLICATIONS publishes books about the American Colonial era, the Revolutionary War, the Civil War, and other important topics. For a complete list of titles, please visit our website at:

http://thomaspublications.com

Or write to:

THOMAS PUBLICATIONS
P.O. Box 3031
Gettysburg, PA 17325

WARNER
FIREARMS COMPANY
Longmeadow Road

Springfield, Mass.